STUDY SKILLS IN ENGLISH

Academic Writing Course

R. R. Jordan

NEW EDITION

LONGMAN

Addison Wesley Longman Limited
Edinburgh Gate, Harlow,
Essex CM20 2JE England
and Associated Companies throughout the World.

© R.R. Jordan 1980, 1990

This edition published by Addison Wesley Longman Ltd 1996

ISBN 0-17-556624-0
Fifth impression 1997

Produced through Longman Malaysia, GPS

Acknowledgements

I am grateful to the following colleagues for their comments on pilot versions of the material and for some ideas which have been incorporated in this course: Gerry Abbott, Ian Anderson, Clare and Mike Beaumont, Graham Cawood, Richard Cullen, Ken James, Jane Jordan, Alan Matthews, Teresa O'Brien, Donald Sim, Richard Walker, Molly Winder, and Peter Wingard. I am indebted to Alan Matthews for kindly providing most of Appendix 6.

In particular, I am grateful to my colleague, June O'Brien, for many useful suggestions for the revised edition.

I am also grateful to numerous overseas students at the University of Manchester for whom most of the material in this course was originally composed.

I wish to express my gratitude to Marilyn Oates for typing the manuscript of the revised edition.

Grateful acknowledgements are made to the following for ideas:
'What Are Science Students Expected to Write?' – J. Friederichs & H. D. Pierson – in *ELT Journal*, Vol. XXXV No. 4, July 1981. 'Essay Examination Prompts and the Teaching of Academic Writing' – D. Horowitz – in *English for Specific Purposes*, Vol. 5 No. 2, 1986. 'Answering Examination Questions' – P. M. Howe – Collins ELT 1983. 'Writing Theses and Dissertations' – J. P. Ryan – University of Manchester 1982. 'The care and maintenance of hedges' – J. Skelton – in *ELT Journal*, Vol. 42 No. 1, January 1988. 'Examining Examination Papers' – J. Swales – in *English Language Research Journal*, No. 3, 1982.

I am grateful to the following for permission to reproduce or make use of copyright material: Unit 2: 'bottle diagram' – based on *Plastics* – Macdonald Junior Reference Library 1969. Unit 6: 'What is language?' – adapted from *The Story of Language*, C. L. Barber – Pan 1964. Unit 7: 'The classification of birds' – adapted from *The Book of British Birds*, Drive Publications Ltd. 1969 and *Ornithology: An Introduction*, Austin L. Rand – Penguin 1974. Unit 9: 'Climate' – adapted from *The Doomsday Book*, G. Rattray Taylor – Thames and Hudson 1970. Unit 10: 'A survey of unemployment' – based on *Illustrated Economics*, Peter Donaldson – B.B.C.; 'Adjusting to higher education' – adapted from *Teaching and Learning in Higher Education* – R. Beard and J. Hartley – Harper & Row, 4th edition, 1984. Unit 11: *Chart 1* – schools – Statistics of Schools: D.E.S.; *Graph 1* 'Marriages in England and Wales' – adapted from 'Marriage and divorce statistics' – O.P.C.S.: HMSO; *Diagram 1:* 'Percentage of households with certain durable goods (GB)' – Britain: HMSO.
Unit 12: 'Advantages and Disadvantages of the Lecturing Method' – adapted from *Teaching and Learning in Higher Education*, Ruth Beard – Penguin 1972. Unit 13: 'Health' text – adapted from *Living Well: The People Maintenance Manual*, ed. Jack Tresidder – Mitchell Beazley 1977. Unit 12 Key: Notes on the Exercises: text quoted from *Teaching and Learning in Higher Education*, Ruth Beard – Penguin 1972.

Photographs

Stuart Boreham © page 52; Bruce Coleman Ltd. pages 38(t), 44(cl,br), 49(b), 57(bl inset, br); S & R Greenhill pages 42(t,cb), 62, 69(t); Robert Harding Picture Library page 49(t); Hulton Picture Company page 28; Gwenan Morgan page 76; NHPA page 44(cr,bl); Network page 42(ct,bl); Oxford Scientific Films pages 44(t), 57(bl); Panos Pictures page 59; Rapporfoto page 27; Science Photo Library page 49(t); Ian Williams page 38(b).
All other photographs by John Walmsley.
Cover photograph The Ancient Art and Architecture Collection.

By the same author:
A Handbook for English Language Assistants (with R. Mackay, Collins 1976)
Listening Comprehension and Note-Taking Course (with K. James and A. J. Matthews, Collins 1979)
Reading in a Second Language (with R. Mackay and B. Barkman, Newbury House 1979)
Looking for Information (Longman 1980)
Figures in Language: Describe and Draw (Collins 1982)
Case Studies in ELT (editor, Collins 1983)
Active Listening (Collins 1984)
Developing Reference Skills (with Teresa O'Brien, Collins 1985)
Language for Economics (with F. I. Nixson, Collins 1986)

Design: Gregor Arthur
Cover Artwork: Douglas Williamson

Photocopying

For Jane

List of Contents

Guide to using the book

The aim of the Course	1 To enable non-native speakers of English who wish to follow a course in the medium of English at tertiary level to express themselves coherently in writing.
	2 To provide samples of academic writing and appropriate practice material for such students and also for those students who need to write essays or reports in English at an intermediate to advanced level.
	3 To act as a revision course for students who have previously learned English as a foreign language at school and who probably learned English with the sentence as the grammatical unit. These students may now need to write in English for academic purposes.
The organisation of the Course	The book is divided into two parts: **a** Functions of Written English and **b** Appendices.
Functions of Written English	The grammatical features of English have been organised into language functions that are used to express a particular notion or idea. Written practice is given at different levels within each unit. A *Key* to the exercises is included at the end of the book (page 127).
Appendices	These act as a bank of reference material which contains information and examples generally useful to the student when he/she is writing. Students should familiarise themselves with the contents of the Appendices before commencing the units. In particular, they should look at *Appendix 1: Accuracy: Awareness and Correction* (page 93). This contains an overview of a number of areas of writing difficulty together with exercises for practice in these areas. Some students would benefit from doing these exercises before beginning the units.
	The book is concerned with aspects of writing at all the different levels: the details of spelling and punctuation, the use of grammatical constructions, and the appropriate style for academic writing.

Using the book

The *units* should be worked through in sequence. The *Appendices* should be referred to when necessary. The *Key* should be checked after each exercise.

The units are organised as follows: each of the units has either two or three stages which are graded in the amount of help and guidance they give. All the units except the last one conclude with a *Structure and Vocabulary Aid* to provide assistance with the words and grammatical constructions needed in that unit. The *Key* at the end of the book (page 127) provides additional comments on the exercises and answers to most of the exercises. Normally, the answers to each exercise should be checked before proceeding to the next exercise.

To the teacher: suggestions

1 In a number of the units there are blank-filling exercises to be done after reading a text. These can be used with some flexibility: students who have difficulty could look at the text again or at the same time as they are writing. Other students could do the exercises without referring back to the text. Advanced students could try to do the exercises *before* looking at the text. In other words, they would be trying to anticipate or predict the language needed from the context of the sentence.

2 Some groups of students may be studying the same academic subject e.g. one of the sciences, social sciences, and so on. If this is the case, then it would be helpful if you could devise some questions related to their specific subject at the end of Stage 3 for each unit.

3 Some students may need practice in writing quickly, especially if they are preparing for an examination in which a limited time is given to answer questions or write an essay. Such students could be given a certain time limit in which to write some of the exercises, particularly those in Stage 3 in the later units. Suitable questions could be composed, making use of the *Glossary* in *Appendix 10* (page 125).

4 The questionnaires on pages 90 to 92 may be photocopied for students to complete.

5 Several discussion activities have been included, and students are encouraged to compare and discuss their answers with other students. The purpose is to raise the level of awareness of students of certain aspects of written English.

Pyramid Discussion

At the end of Unit 2, Stage 3, (page 18) there is an activity called 'Pyramid Discussion'.

The purpose of this discussion activity is to raise the students' awareness of the important features of continuous academic writing. It is an activity in which students are encouraged to take part in discussion by gradually increasing the size of the discussion group, starting with the individual, then building up to two students, then four, and then the whole group. The procedure is as follows:

a First, students should individually select three items, as instructed, from the list given in the activity. The order of their three choices is not important.

b Then each student, in turn, should call out the numbers of his/her choices. Write these on the blackboard for all to see.

e.g.	student:	A	B	C	D etc.
	choices:	12	3	4	1
		14	7	7	7
		15	10	12	10

c After this, put the students in pairs so that they have, as far as possible, at least one choice in common (e.g. A and C, B and D above).

d In pairs the students should then try to persuade each other to make changes in their choices so that at the end of a certain time limit (perhaps five minutes) they both agree on three choices. If necessary, they can compromise on new choices or 'trade-off' choices. The pairs' three choices are then noted on the blackboard.

e Pairs should then be placed together who have at least one choice the same . . . and so the procedure continues until all of the class are involved.

f If a pair or group finish their discussion before other groups, they can prepare arguments to defend their choices so that they are ready to meet another group.

g While they are discussing, students will be practising the language of persuasion: agreement, disagreement, suggestion, qualification and compromise.

h At the end of the activity is a suggestion that students can add some advice of their own to the list. This may be done in pairs instead of, or in addition to, individually.

i 13 in the list refers to: clichés, jargon, propaganda, exaggeration, and emotive language. Ask the students if they can give examples of these types of language. If necessary, give examples yourself.

5 Some practice in spelling commonly misspelt words is given in *Appendix 1* Spelling (page 95)
Dictation

One way to give more practice in the spelling of words that cause difficulty is to include them in appropriate sentences and to read them out as a dictation. Some examples are given below of words taken from the list of 40 in the Spelling Recognition exercise (page 95).

a Many students have difficulty finding *accommodation* in the city.
b He *achieved* only half of his aims.
c This regulation is not *applicable* to me!
d She arrived at the *beginning* of October.

e Usually some *choice* is given in examination questions.
f In seminars there may be some *criticism* of one's views.
g Economic *Development* is a popular subject with students.
h By the end of term his language problems had *disappeared*.
i The class was *divided* into three groups.
j In language learning, some *emphasis* should be put on accuracy.

1 Note the following words: they are also commonly misspelt.

acquire	category	interrupt	preferring
aggression	consistent	liaison	procedure
ancillary	definite	maintenance	relevant
argument	environment	occasion	repetition
assimilation	inferred	omission	respectively
auxiliary	integration	permissible	

2 A general spelling rule that is useful:
'i' before 'e' except after 'c' e.g. bel*ie*f; c*ei*ling
Some exceptions: ancient, feint, foreign, neighbour, reign

3 Spelling of the sound – *seed*
   (a) only 1 word – *sede* = supersede
   (b) only 3 words – *ceed* = exceed, proceed, succeed
   (c) the rest = – *cede* = precede, etc.

References

The following will be found useful for further explanation and practice:

Longman Dictionary of Common Errors – J. B. Heaton and N. D. Turton – Longman
A Communicative Grammar of English – G. Leech and J. Svartvik – Longman
An Intermediate English Practice Book – S. Pit Corder – Longman
A Grammar of Contemporary English – Quirk, Greenbaum, Leech and Svartvik – Longman
Practical English Usage – M. Swan – O.U.P.
A Practical English Grammar – A. J. Thomson and A. V. Martinet – O.U.P.
Grammar in Context – Hugh Gethin – Collins ELT

Functions of Written English

The notes on the exercises and the answers are in the Key at the end of the book (page 127).

Unit 1   Structure and Cohesion

This unit is concerned with the general organisation of a piece of academic writing (e.g. a report, an essay, an assignment, a project), its structure and particularly the way in which the different parts are linked together. The plan below of a piece of writing, in this case an essay, will help to explain the overall structure.

Stage 1   Structure

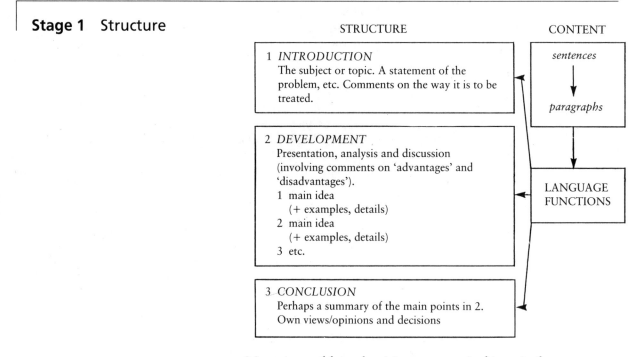

Most pieces of formal writing are organised in a similar way — introduction; development of main ideas or arguments; conclusions. Each part of the writing will consist of language functions: particular uses and structures of the language organised according to the specific purpose that the writer has in mind in wishing to communicate his ideas etc. to other people — describing, defining, exemplifying, classifying etc.

Each language function consists of sentences and/or paragraphs that are joined together or linked by connectives (words or phrases that indicate a logical relationship). These language functions will be examined in detail in the following units. In the rest of this unit we shall look at the linking of sentences by means of *connectives*.

Stage 2   Connectives

A piece of writing or text will often have the following structure:

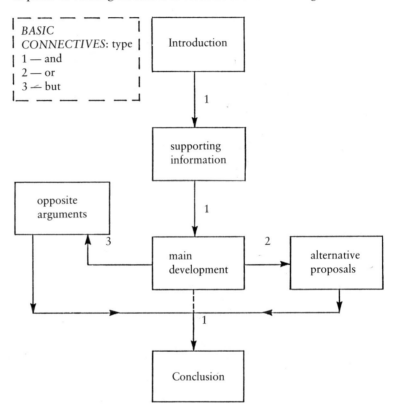

1   The discussion, argument, or comment in the development of the topic may be very straightforward, in which case ideas will be added together one after the other. The basic connective 1 *and* is used here. (A number of connectives have a similar or related meaning to *and*.)

2   Sometimes the comments may be expressed in another way, or an alternative proposal may be made. This is represented by the basic connective 2 *or*. (A number of other connectives have a similar meaning.) After the alternative has been considered, the main argument will continue.

3   There are also occasions in arguments etc. when the opposite is considered or referred to. This is represented by the basic connective 3 *but*. (There are also a number of other connectives with a similar meaning.) After the opposite or opposing view has been considered, the main argument is continued.

A list of the connectives divided into the main groups of *and*, *or, but* is contained in *Appendix 8: Connectives* (page 118).

Exercises

In the following exercises practice is given in some examples of the three main groups of connectives.

1 'And' type: Connectives of Result

Look at the following example:

	therefore, *as a result,* *accordingly,*	
He passed his examinations;	*consequently,* *thus,* *hence,*	he had some good news to tell his parents.

Because he passed his examinations,

Note: The connectives (in *italics*) join a cause ('he passed his examinations') with a result, effect or consequence ('he had some good news to tell his parents').

Exercise 1a

To the following sentences add (*a*) a suitable connective from the list above, and (*b*) an appropriate result, effect or consequence from the list below.

1 Many students find it difficult to read newspapers in English . . .
_____

2 Most students living abroad are interested in news of their own country . . . _____

3 When a student goes abroad to study he/she may have to complete about twelve different forms . . . _____
_____

Result, Effect or Consequence:

a British news is found to be of most interest.
b they usually read the international news first in the newspapers.
c an average of five books per month are read.
d not many read one regularly.
e it is useful to be able to answer questions briefly.

Exercise 1b

Complete the following by adding a suitable ending of your own.

4 The lecture was very difficult to understand. Consequently, ____
_____

5 Carlos was only able to read very slowly in English. Therefore,
_____

2 'Or' type: Connectives of Reformulation

Look at the following example:

| He said that he had kept the library book for several years. | *In other words* / *To put it more simply,* / *It would be better to say* | he had stolen it. |

Note: The connectives (in *italics*) introduce a reformulation of what has come before. The reformulation appears in different words and is used to make the idea clearer or to explain or modify it.

Exercise 2a
To the following sentences add (*a*) a suitable connective from the list above, and (*b*) an appropriate reformulation from the list below.

1 Maria is rather slow at learning . . . _____

2 Helen finds languages quite easy . . . _____

3 Anna speaks English like a native-speaker . . . _____

Reformulation:
a she speaks it excellently.
b she speaks slowly,
c she is taking a long time to improve her English.
d she has little difficulty in learning English.
e she speaks it with great difficulty.

Exercise 2b
Complete the following by adding a suitable ending of your own.

4 Margaret is bilingual. In other words, _____

5 Some people say that if you are good at music you will also be good at learning languages. In other words, _____

3 'But' type: Connectives of Concession

Look at the following example:

| The time available for discussion was very limited. | *However,* / *Nevertheless,* / *Nonetheless,* / *Yet,* / *In spite of that,* / *All the same,* | it was still possible to produce some interesting arguments. |

Note: The connectives (in *italics*) indicate the surprising nature of what follows in view of what was said before; a kind of contrast is indicated.

Exercise 3a
To the following sentences add (*a*) a suitable connective from the list above, and (*b*) an appropriate concession (or contrast) from the list over the page.

1 Some of the examination questions were very difficult . . . _____

2 There was only limited money available for research . . . _____

3 The project was very complicated . . . _____

_____

Concession:
a Dimitrios was not able to do it.
b Juan succeeded in completing it in time.
c Abdul was able to obtain a grant.
d Oscar did not manage to complete them.
e Ali managed to answer them satisfactorily.

Exercise 3b
Complete the following by adding a suitable ending of your own.
4 It seemed likely that he would fail the test. However, _____

_____

5 There were a number of good reasons why he should not finish
the experiment. Nevertheless, _____

_____

Now turn to page 127 and check your answers.
For a list of the connectives and more information turn to
Appendix 8: Connectives (page 118).

Unit 2 Description: Process and Procedure

When we describe a process or procedure, we often use the present passive tense (is/are + verb stem + ed e.g. *it is manufactured*) to give a general description.

When we report a *particular procedure* we are concerned with only one particular occasion in the past; then we often use the past passive tense (was/were + verb stem + ed e.g. *it was heated*).

A description that does not involve a process or procedure is often written in the present simple active tense (verb stem + s e.g. *it comprises*).

Sequence, or order, is important in both describing a process or reporting a procedure.

Stage 1
General Description

1a Read the following carefully. Note particularly the verb forms that are used: some of the present passive verb forms have been underlined.

How paper is made
Paper is made from wood, and many of the world's paper mills are found in those countries which have great forests — Canada, Sweden and Finland.
The trees are felled or cut down.
The branches and leaves are removed.
The trees are transported to the sawmill.
The bark is stripped from the trunks.
The trunks are sawn into logs.
They are conveyed to the paper mill.
They are placed in the shredder.
They are cut into small chips.
They are mixed with water and acid.
They are heated and crushed to a heavy pulp.
This wood pulp is cleaned.
It is also chemically bleached to whiten it.
It is passed through rollers to flatten it.
Sheets of wet paper are produced.
The water is removed from the sheets.
These sheets are pressed, dried and refined until the finished paper is produced.

b Read carefully through the text again and underline any further verbs in the present passive tense.

2a When describing a process, sequence markers, e.g. *first, then, next, finally* . . . are often used (see *Appendix 8: Connectives, Section 1*, page 118). They help to link the sentences.

b Sometimes, in order to avoid repeating a subject, a relative pronoun and relative clause are used.

e.g. The bark is stripped from *the trunks. The trunks* are sawn into logs.

becomes:

The bark is stripped from *the trunks which* are sawn into logs.

c Some of the sentences from the text have been joined together below to form a paragraph. Spaces have been left in the sentences. In the spaces write an appropriate verb (and sometimes preposition), and, if suitable, a relative pronoun.

First, the logs _____ in the shredder. Then they _____ into small chips _____ water and acid. Next they _____ to a heavy pulp ____ _____ . It _____ also chemically _____ _____ to whiten it. After this, it _____ rollers to flatten it. Then, sheets of wet paper _____ ____. Finally, the water _____ from the sheets _____ until the finished paper _____.

3 Look at the sequence of pictures below. Underneath there are a number of sentences describing how a breakfast cereal is made. The sentences are in the wrong order. Write them out in the correct order using the sequence of pictures to help you.

How a breakfast cereal is made

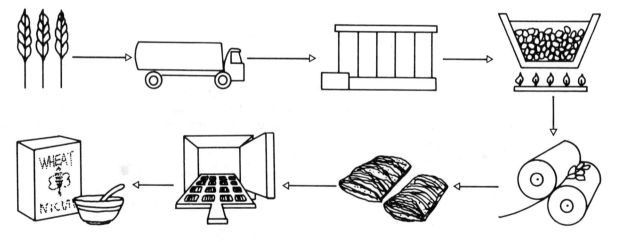

a It is stored in the silos.
b These are woven into biscuits.
c The wheat is harvested from the field.
d Each biscuit is baked until brown.
e It is cut in thin strips.
f The grain is cooked to soften it.
g It is packed ready to be eaten.
h The wheat grain is transported to the silos.

4 Look carefully at the diagram on page 15 of the stages of manufacture of glass bottles. Six boxes have been numbered and left empty. Now read carefully the sentences next to the diagram. They are in the *wrong* order and are not complete.

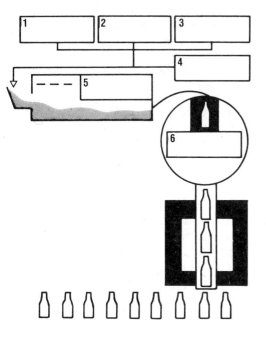

a Complete the sentences by putting the verb (given at the end of each sentence) in the appropriate passive form.
b Write the sentences in the *correct* order.
c Join them together by means of sequence markers (e.g. *then, next*).
d Finally, from the information in the sentences, write the correct names in the six boxes in the diagram.

How glass bottles are made
a It _____ into bottles in the mould. (shape).
b Sometimes broken glass _____. (add)
c The bottles _____ to strengthen the glass. (reheat and cool)
d Glass _____ from sand, limestone, and soda ash. (make)
e They are ready _____ . (use)
f Glass _____. (produce)
g This mixture _____ strongly in a furnace. (heat)
h These three materials _____ together in the right proportions. (mix)

Stage 2
Specific Procedure

1 Look at the following table carefully.

Writing in English: Manchester University (50 students)

% students	type of writing	(average) frequency	(average) length
52	essay	5 per term	2000 words
34	report	2 per term	4000 words
14	dissertation	1 per year	8000 words
12	thesis	1 after 2–3 years	300–1000 pages

The information in the table can be described (as an alternative to using the table). Notice the construction of the following sentence:

52% of the students wrote essays, *of an* average frequency *of 5* per term, *of an* average length of 2000 words.

Now read the following paragraph, which describes some of the information contained in the table. Complete the spaces with information from the table.

A survey was conducted among _____ overseas postgraduate students at _____. The purpose of the survey was to discover the type, _____ and _____ of academic writing that was expected of the students by their supervisors or tutors. _____ of the students _____ reports, of an _____ 2 per term, _____ average length _____.

2 Below the steps or stages in conducting a survey are given. In the spaces in each sentence write an appropriate verb from the following list. Put the verbs in the past passive tense e.g. *was/were asked*.

Verbs: request, collect, carry out, publish, analyse, distribute

a A survey _____ among 50 students.
b First, questionnaires _____ to the students.
c Then the students _____ to write answers to the questions.
d After this, the completed questionnaires _____ .
e Next, the answers _____ .
f Finally, the results _____ .

Note: See Unit 15 (page 88) for conducting an actual survey.

Stage 3   Advice

1 Read carefully the following description of the procedure for writing an essay. It gives advice in the form of what you *should* do. (Most of the verbs are in the passive simple conditional.) When you have finished reading do the exercise in **2**.

The Stages of Writing an Essay

First, the topic, subject or question should be thought about carefully: what is required in the essay should be understood. Then a note should be made of ideas, perhaps from knowledge or experience. After this, any books,
5 journals, etc. should be noted that have been recommended, perhaps from a reading list or a bibliography. Then to the list should be added any other books, articles, etc. that are discovered while the recommended books are being found.

Now is the time for the books, chapters, articles, etc. to be
10 read, with a purpose, by appropriate questions being asked that are related to the essay topic or title. Clear notes should be written from the reading. In addition, a record of the sources should be kept so that a bibliography or list of references can be compiled at the end of the essay. Any
15 quotations should be accurately acknowledged: author's surname and initials, year of publication, edition, publisher, place of publication, and page numbers of quotations.

When the notes have been finished they should be looked through in order for an overview of the subject to be
20 obtained. Then the content of the essay should be decided on and how it is to be organised or planned. The material should be carefully selected: there may be too much and some may not be very relevant to the question. The material, or ideas, should be divided into three main sections for the essay: the
25 introduction, the main body, and the conclusion. An outline of the essay should be written, with use being made of headings or sub-headings, if they are appropriate.

The first draft should be written in a suitably formal or academic style. While doing this, the use of colloquial

30 expressions and personal references should be avoided. When it has been completed, the draft should be read critically, and in particular, the organisation, cohesion, and language should be checked. Several questions should be asked about it, for example: Is it clear? Is it concise? Is it
35 comprehensive? Then the draft should be revised and the final draft written — legibly! It should be remembered that first impressions are important.

   Finally, the bibliography should be compiled, using the conventional format: the references should be in strict
40 alphabetical order. Then the bibliography should be added to the end of the essay.

2 All the sentences containing advice ('should') are listed below. Spaces have been left for the verbs. In each space write the appropriate verb, but write it as a direct *instruction* (putting the verb in its imperative form) e.g. *should be finished→finish*.

The Stages of Writing an Essay

a _____ carefully about the topic, subject or question.

b _____ what is required in the essay.

c _____ a note of your ideas, perhaps from your knowledge or experience.

d _____ any books, journals, etc. that have been recommended, perhaps from a reading list or a bibliography.

e _____ to your list any other books, articles, etc. that you discover while finding the recommended books.

f _____ the books, chapters, articles, etc. with a purpose, by asking yourself appropriate questions that are related to the essay topic or title.

g _____ clear notes from your reading.

h _____ a record of your sources so that you can compile your own bibliography or list of references at the end of your essay.

i _____ accurately any quotations: author's surname and initials, year of publication, edition, publisher, place of publication, and page numbers of quotations.

j _____ through your notes when you have finished in order to obtain an overview of the subject.

k _____ on the content of your essay and how you want to organise it, in other words, plan it.

l _____ your material carefully: you may have too much and some may not be very relevant to the question.

m _____ your material, or ideas, into three main sections for the essay: the

Summary of the Stages of Writing an Essay

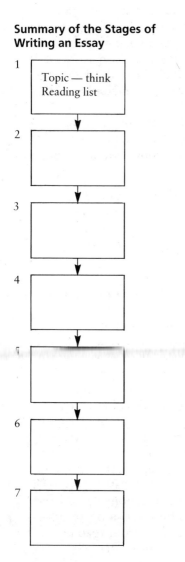

n _____ introduction, the main body, and the conclusion.

an outline of the essay, making use of headings or sub-headings, if they are appropriate.

o _____ the first draft, in a suitably formal or academic style.

p _____ the use of colloquial expressions and personal references.

q _____ the draft critically, in particular checking the organisation, cohesion and language.

r _____ yourself several questions about it, for example: Is it clear? Is it concise? Is it comprehensive?

s _____ the draft.

t _____ the final draft.

u _____ sure it is legible!

v _____ first impressions are important.

w _____ your bibliography, using the conventional format.

x _____ that your references are in strict alphabetical order.

y _____ the bibliography to the end of your essay.

3 Read through 'The Stages of Writing an Essay' again. Decide what you consider to be the most important stages or advice. In very brief note form summarise the stages by filling in the boxes in the diagram. The first one has been done for you (you may change it if you do not agree with it).

Either: Before beginning, discuss with the student next to you what you both consider to be the most important stages. Do you agree with each other?

Or: After you have finished, compare your summary diagram with the student next to you and discuss any differences.

Pyramid Discussion
Writing an essay or report

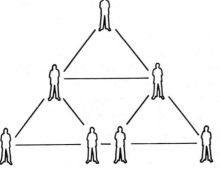

Individually select the three most important pieces of advice, from the list below, that you think will help to improve a student's academic writing. The order of the three choices is not important.

1 Write precisely: clearly, accurately and explicitly.
2 Use correct language: grammar, vocabulary, spelling etc.
3 Organise the writing carefully: introduction, main body, and conclusion.
4 Write legibly: handwriting should be easy to read.
5 Write in an academic style: impersonally, without using colloquial language.
6 Write concisely, and avoid very long sentences.
7 Adopt appropriate attitudes: be rational, critical, honest and objective.

8 Carefully paragraph the writing.

9 Include variety in the writing: avoid too much repetition.

10 Check details carefully, both of content and of language.

11 Ensure that the opening paragraph is not too long and that it creates a good impression.

12 Pay as much attention to the conclusion as to the introduction.

13 Avoid the use of clichés, jargon, propaganda, exaggeration, and emotive language.

14 Ensure that ideas and items are arranged in a logical sequence and are logically connected.

15 Always acknowledge the source of quotations and paraphrases.

Finally add some advice of your own that is not covered in the list above.

Note: Information about organising a Pyramid Discussion in the classroom is given in *Guide to using the book* (page 5).

Structure and Vocabulary Aid

A Commonly used verb tenses, with examples.

Present Simple (Active) it carries/they carry	Present Simple (Passive) it is carried/they are carried

Past Simple (Active) it carried/they carried	Past Simple (Passive) it was carried/they were carried

Passive Simple Conditional it should be given/they should be given	Imperative/instruction give

B **Relative pronouns** and *relative clauses*

1 **Who** (and **that**) refers to persons.
2 **Which/that** refer to things.
3 **Whose** refers to the possessive of persons.
4 **Whom** refers to persons and is often used with a preposition.

Examples:

1 My supervisor **who** *seems very young* has just been promoted to head of department.
2 The article **which** (or **that**) *I have just finished reading* is very clearly written.
3 The research **that** (or **which**) *I finished last year* has just been published.
4 The lecturer **whose** *name I always forget* was as boring as usual this morning.
5 The student **with whom** *I share a room* is very noisy (*formal*). (*informal* = The student I share a room with is very noisy.)

Unit 3   Description: Physical

In academic writing, physical description may occur in a number of disciplines or subjects. A description of people, family relationships, occupations and institutions might occur in social or physical anthropology or sociology. A description of apparatus and equipment might occur in the various sciences. For nearly all these descriptions the present simple active tense (e.g. *she wears/they wear*) and present simple passive tense (e.g. *it is described/ they are described*) are commonly used. The following stages concentrate on describing countries.

Stage 1
The United Kingdom

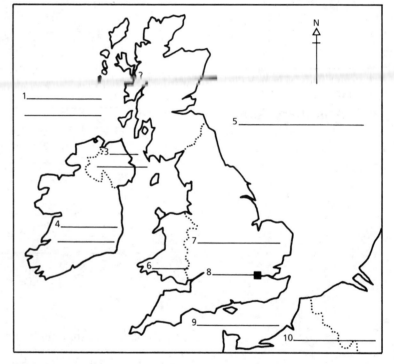

Read the following paragraph carefully and then do the exercise.

The United Kingdom

Great Britain (G.B.) is an island that lies off the north-west coast of Europe. The nearest country is France which is 20 miles away and from which Great Britain is separated by the English Channel. The island is surrounded by the Atlantic
5 Ocean to the west, and the North Sea to the east. It comprises the mainlands of England, Wales and Scotland, that is, three countries. Scotland is in the north, while Wales is in the west. Ireland, which is also an island, lies off the west coast of Great Britain. It consists of Northern Ireland and the
10 Irish Republic. Great Britain together with Northern Ireland constitutes the United Kingdom (U.K.). Thus, the United

Kingdom is composed of four countries. The largest of these is England which is divided into 45 administrative counties. The capital city is London which is situated in south-east
15 England.

1 From the information above write the names of the places next to the numbers in the map.

Now continue to read about the United Kingdom.

The United Kingdom has a total area of about 244,100 square kilometres. About 70% of the land area is devoted to agriculture, about 7% is wasteland, moorland and mountains, about 13% is devoted to urban development, and 10% is
20 forest and woodland. The northern and western regions of Great Britain, that is Scotland and Wales, are mainly mountainous and hilly. Parts of the north-west and centre of England also consist of mountains and hills.
    Great Britain, or Britain, as it is usually called, has a
25 generally mild and temperate climate. It is, however, subject to frequent changes. It has an average annual rainfall of a little over 40 inches (101.6 cm), while England alone has about 34 inches (85.4 cm).
    In mid 1988 the estimated population of the United
30 Kingdom was 57 million. The density of population was approximately 233 people per square km., but in England the density was higher: there were 363 people per square km. In the United Kingdom English is the language which is predominantly spoken. In Wales, however, Welsh is the first
35 language of the majority of the population in most of the western counties. It was spoken by 19% of the population of Wales in 1981. Both English and Welsh are official languages in Wales. In Scotland only about 80,000 people in 1981 spoke the Scottish form of Gaelic. The predominant religion in
40 Britain is Christianity. Its main branches are the Church of England, the Church in Wales, the Church of Scotland, the Roman Catholic Church, and the Methodist Church.

2 Read through the whole passage again from the beginning ('Great Britain is an island . . .'). When you have finished, complete the following summary of the passage by using appropriate verb forms in the spaces. Sometimes a preposition is needed as well.

Great Britain is an island that (1) _____ the Atlantic Ocean and the North Sea. It (2) _____ the mainlands of England, Wales and Scotland. Ireland (3) _____ the west coast of Great Britain. It (4) _____ Northern Ireland and the Irish Republic. The United Kingdom (5) _____ Britain together with Northern Ireland. The capital city is London which (6) _____ south-east England.
    In 1988 the population of the United Kingdom (7) _____ _____ 57 million. The density of population (8) _____ _____ 233 people per square km. In England there (9) _____ 363 people per square km. In the United Kingdom English is the language which (10) _____

predominantly _____ . In Wales, Welsh (11) _____ 19% of the population in 1981. In Scotland 80,000 people in 1981 (12) _____ the Scottish form of Gaelic.

Stage 2 Other Countries

1 Look carefully at the map of Iceland below and then at the table of information. Then write a description of Iceland organised in a similar way to the description of the United Kingdom. Write four short paragraphs on:

    location
    size and physical background
    climate
    population, language, and religion

Where possible use the same verbs, verb tenses and vocabulary as in the description of the United Kingdom. Check the *Structure and Vocabulary Aid* (page 23).

Iceland

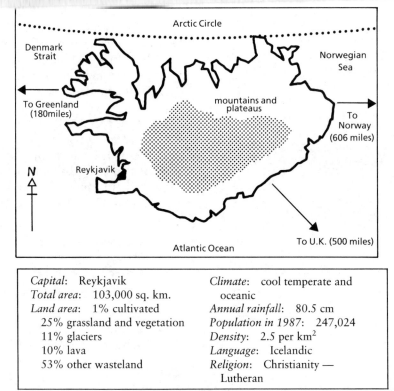

Capital: Reykjavik	*Climate*: cool temperate and oceanic
Total area: 103,000 sq. km.	
Land area: 1% cultivated	*Annual rainfall*: 80.5 cm
25% grassland and vegetation	*Population in 1987*: 247,024
11% glaciers	*Density*: 2.5 per km^2
10% lava	*Language*: Icelandic
53% other wasteland	*Religion*: Christianity — Lutheran

2 Now write a brief account of your country. Write four paragraphs on:

    location
    size and physical background
    climate
    population, language, and religion

If you do not know the exact figures, guess or write in general terms. As far as possible use the description of the United Kingdom as a guide. Make use of the *Structure and Vocabulary Aid* which follows to help you with your writing.

Structure and Vocabulary Aid
A Vocabulary: Countries

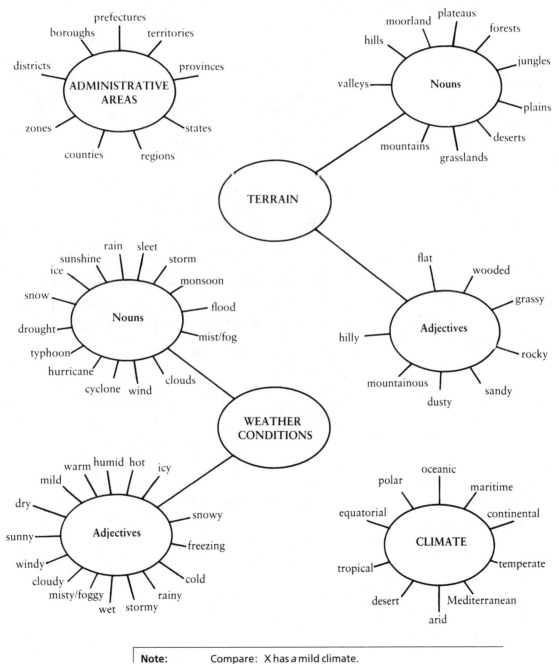

Note: Compare: X has a mild climate.
X has mild weather.

B Compass points (and adjectives)

North
(northern)

North-West
(north-western)

North-East
(north-eastern)

West
(western)

East
(eastern)

South-West
(south-western)

South-East
(south-eastern)

South
(southern)

C Location

x is situated/located

– in . . .
– to . . .
– on . . .

Y

country

Z

X

N

e.g. X is *in the south* of the country.
   Y is *to the north* of the country.
   The north of the country is cold.
         on/near the equator.
         on/near the coast/sea.
         inland.
   Z is a neighbouring adjacent country.

lies (to lie) is used for islands. For mainland (joined to a continent) we would use *is situated* in referring to location.

Verbs to describe the composition of a country:

X
comprise(s) . . .
consist(s) of . . .
constitute(s) . . .
is composed of . . .
} (notice the use and differences)

Approximation:

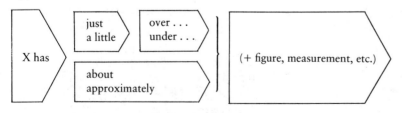

X has

just
a little

over . . .
under . . .

about
approximately

(+ figure, measurement, etc.)

Qualification:

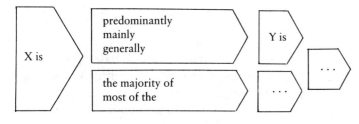

D 'The' with names of countries, rivers and seas

1 *The* is *not* used with names of continents (e.g. Europe, not *the* Europe) though it is used with some other geographical areas (e.g. *the* Middle East, *the* Far East).
2 *The* + Republic of . . . (e.g. *the* Republic of France).
3 *The* + country names in the plural (e.g. *the* United States of America, *the* U.K., *the* U.S.S.R., *the* West Indies).
4 Other country names are *not* used with *the* (e.g. *Denmark*).
5 *The* + names of oceans, seas, rivers (e.g. *the* Atlantic Ocean, *the* Mediterranean, *the* Tigris) but *not* with names of lakes (e.g. *Lake Baikal*).
6 *The* + names of mountain ranges (e.g. *the* Alps, *the* Himalayas).

1 Can you think of any more words to add to the above lists? Think particularly of your own country.
2 Are there any more categories or groups of words that you would find useful? If so, try to make lists similar to the above.

Unit 4 Narrative

The introduction to many pieces of academic writing contains some kind of historical background or development. This is usually in the form of narrative: an account or description of events in the past which entails following a time sequence or chronological order (i.e. earliest first). Verb forms commonly used are the simple past active (e.g. *it organised*), simple past passive (e.g. *it was created*), and past perfect active (e.g. *it had developed*).

Stage 1   E.E.C (notes)

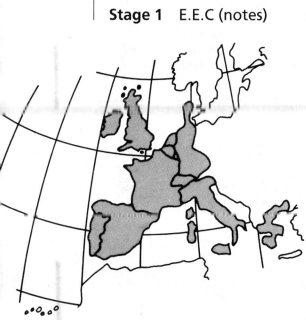

1   Read the following carefully. Notice the structure, time sequence, date forms and prepositions, and the verb forms used.

The European Economic Community (E.E.C. or Common Market — also called The European Community — E.C.)

The beginnings of the E.E.C. date from May 9th 1950, when Robert Schuman, France's Foreign Minister, proposed that
5   France and Germany should combine their coal and steel industries under an independent, 'supranational' authority. This led to the establishment of the
10   European Coal and Steel Community (E.C.S.C.) in 1952. In addition to France and Germany, Belgium, Italy, Luxemburg and the Netherlands also became
15   members.
　　The E.C.S.C. was a step towards economic integration in Europe and led to the Treaty of Rome which was signed on
20   March 25th 1957. This established the E.E.C. with the same six member states as in the E.C.S.C. In 1973 the U.K., Denmark and the Republic of Ireland became
25   members; Greece, Spain and Portugal joined in the 1980s.

beginnings/origins
date from/go back to . . .

led to the establishment/
founding/creation/setting
up/of . . .
in 1952

led to/ resulted in . . .
on March 25th
established/created/set up . . .
up . . .

in 1973

became members/joined
in the 1980s.

2   Now make very brief notes of the most important items of information in the passage.

Stage 2 U.N. (notes)

1 Read through the passage below, then write an appropriate word in each of the spaces.

The United Nations

The _____ of the U.N. can _____ traced back _____ the League of Nations. This _____ an international _____ which _____ created _____ the Treaty of Versailles _____ 1920 with the purpose _____ achieving world peace. Before 1930, the League, from its Geneva headquarters, _____ international conferences and did useful humanitarian work. _____, it failed _____ deal effectively _____ international aggression _____ the 1930s. The League _____ formally closed _____ 1946 and _____ superseded _____ the United Nations.

The U.N. was _____ on 24th October 1945, when the U.N. Charter _____ ratified _____ the 51 founder member countries. Almost _____ the countries of the _____ are now members; 159 in all.

The U.N. was _____ to maintain international peace, and to encourage international co-operation to overcome economic, social, cultural and humanitarian problems. Apart _____ the _____ organs of the U.N. (e.g. The General Assembly, The Security Council etc.), _____ of the U.N.'s work is done _____ its specialised bodies _____ agencies. _____ of the best _____ are, perhaps, the FAO, ILO, IMF, WHO, UNESCO and UNICEF.

Discuss possible alternative answers. When the text is complete, continue with the following exercise.

2 Now make very brief notes of the most important items of information in the passage.

Stage 3
Universities (expanded notes)

1 Below is a passage tracing the development of universities. Read it through. When you have finished reading it do exercise 2 which follows the passage.

The Development of Universities

The word 'university' comes from the Latin word 'universitas', meaning 'the whole'. Later, in Latin legal language 'universitas' meant 'a society, guild or corporation'. Thus, in mediaeval academic use the word meant an
5 association of teachers and scholars. The modern definition of a university is 'an institution that teaches and examines students in many branches of advanced learning, awarding degrees and providing facilities for academic research'.

The origins of universities can be traced back to the Middle
10 Ages, especially the 12–14th centuries. In the early 12th
century, long before universities were organised in the
modern sense, students gathered together for higher studies
at certain centres of learning. The earliest centres in Europe
were at Bologna in Italy, for law, founded in 1088; Salerno in
15 Italy for medicine; and Paris, France, for philosophy and
theology, founded in 1150. Other early ones in Europe were
at Prague, Czechoslovakia, founded in 1348; Vienna, Austria,
founded in 1365; and Heidelberg, Germany, founded in 1386.

The first universities in England were established at Oxford
20 in 1185 and at Cambridge in 1209. The first Scottish university
was founded at St. Andrews in 1412. By comparison, the
oldest universities in the U.S.A. are at Harvard, founded in
1636, and Yale, established in 1701.

In the fifteenth and sixteenth centuries, three more
25 universities were founded in Scotland: at Glasgow in 1415,
Aberdeen in 1494, and Edinburgh in 1582. The next English
university to be founded was not until the nineteenth century
— London, in 1836. This was followed, later in the nineteenth
and early twentieth centuries, by the foundation of several
30 civic universities. These had developed from provincial
colleges which were mainly situated in industrial areas.
Manchester, for example, received its charter in 1880, and
Birmingham in 1900. In addition, the federal University of
Wales was established in 1893 comprising three colleges.

35 Several other civic universities were founded in the 1940s
and 1950s, such as Nottingham in 1948, Southampton in 1954
and Exeter in 1957. However, it was in the 1960s that the
largest single expansion of higher education took place in
Britain. This expansion took three basic forms: existing
40 universities were enlarged; new universities were developed
from existing colleges; and seven completely new universities
were founded. The latest, Kent University, in south-east
England, and Warwick, in the Midlands, were both founded
in 1965. Like the other new universities, they are situated
45 away from town centres and are surrounded by parkland and
green fields.

Finance for universities comes from three sources, namely
grants from the government (the largest), fees paid by
students, and donations from private sources. All the British
50 universities, except one, receive some government funding.
The exception is Buckingham, which is Britain's only
independent university, and which received the Royal Charter
in 1983.

One of the latest university developments was the
55 foundation in 1969 of the Open University. It is a non-
residential university which provides part-time degree and
other courses. It uses a combination of correspondence
courses, television and radio broadcasts, and summer schools
organised on a regional basis.

top: Bologna University
centre: Vienna University
bottom: Merton College, Oxford University

2 Below is a summary of the passage in sentences which are given in the wrong order. Put the sentences in the correct order by writing the letters **a–j** next to numbers 1–10.

a The quarter of a century from 1940 to 1965 was the period when there was a big increase in the number of universities in Britain.

b The Open University was founded in 1969.

c The oldest American university was founded in the 17th century.

d One of the original meanings of 'university' was an association of teachers and students.

e There is one private university in Britain: it was established in 1983.

f After three more Scottish universities were established in the 15th and 16th centuries, the next major developments were not until the foundation of a number of civic universities in the nineteenth and early twentieth centuries.

g Oxford and Cambridge are the oldest English universities.

h Government grants are the most important source of university income.

i The first Scottish university was established in the early 15th century.

j There were gatherings of students at centres of learning in Europe between the twelfth and fourteenth centuries.

3 Now make brief notes of the information relating to the development of English universities only. Put the heading *Universities in England* above your notes.

4 Write a brief description in narrative form of the development of universities in your country. It does not matter if you do not know precise dates or details: a rough idea or an approximation will be sufficient. Refer to the *Structure and Vocabulary Aid* (page 30).

5 If you apply for a job or to study at a university etc., you normally fill in an application form or send a *curriculum vitae* (c.v.). This is a brief account (description) of your background and career. Normally it includes your full name, date of birth, and then, under the heading of *education*, a summary of the secondary schools, colleges or universities that you have attended, together with details of examinations passed and certificates and/or degrees awarded. It is usually followed by an account of your employment or career. The information is normally given in chronological order.

Write part of your own c.v. Only include information under the heading of *education* (places of study and awards).

6 Write a letter to a university or a college applying to study there in the next academic year.

Structure and Vocabulary Aid

A Commonly used verb tenses, with examples.

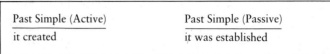

Past Simple (Active)	Past Simple (Passive)
it created	it was established

Past Perfect (Active)
It had developed

B Useful verbs/nouns

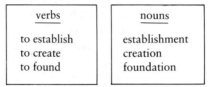

verbs	nouns
to establish	establishment
to create	creation
to found	foundation

C Useful vocabulary for describing post-school education.

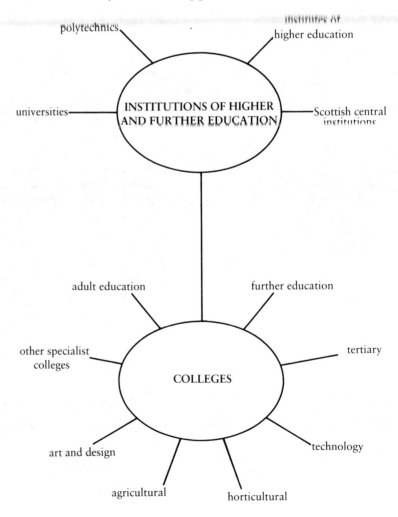

D Useful vocabulary for describing universities.

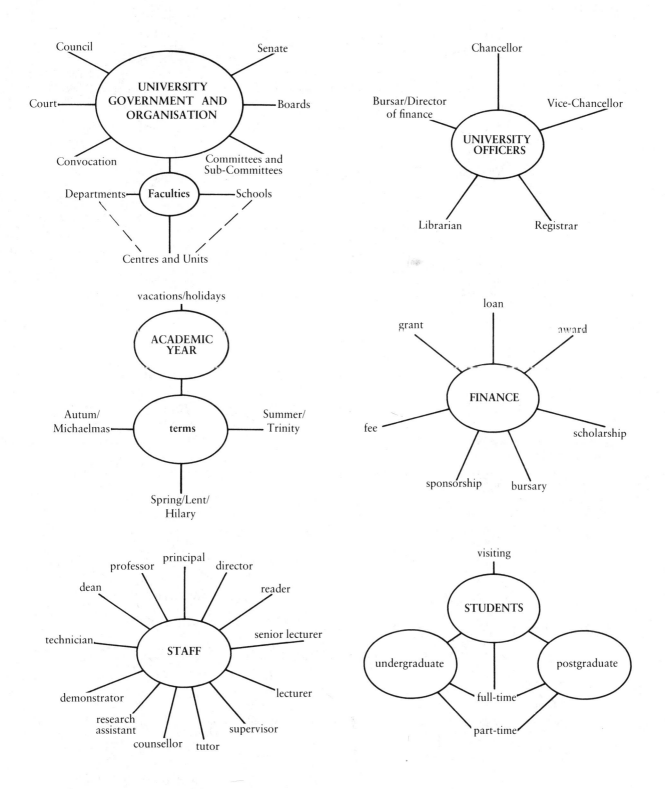

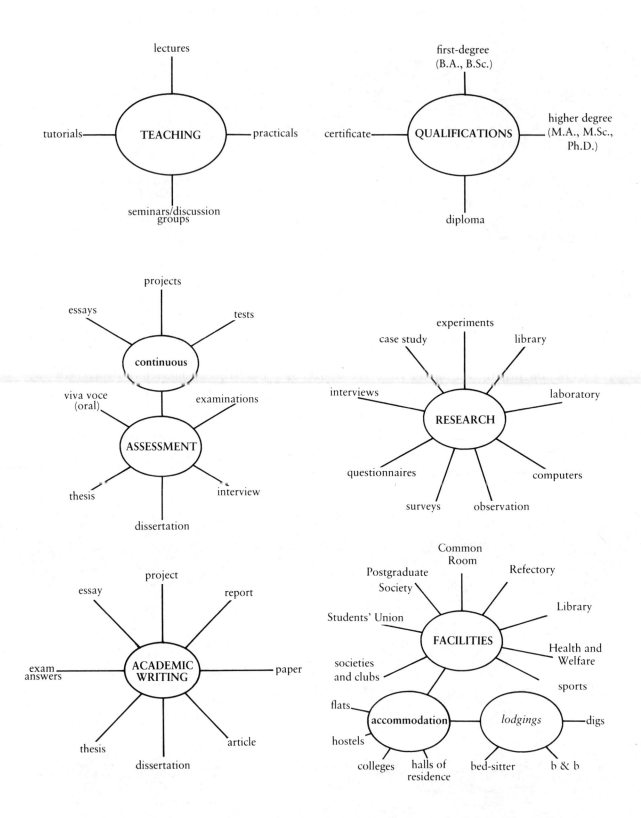

1 Can you think of any more words to add to the above lists?

2 Take the subject *Academic Reading.* Make a list of words for it (types of reading) in the same way as the above.

Unit 5 Definitions

The previous units were concerned with describing things. When we describe things we sometimes need to define them as well, especially in academic writing, so that it is perfectly clear what we mean. We may also need to give examples of what we define, and to classify. These will be covered in the following units.

Stage 1
Simple Definitions

1 If we look in a dictionary for the word 'school' we may find:

school an institution where children are educated

More formally in writing we would put:

A school is an institution where children are educated.

Look at these other examples:

A doctor is a person who gives medical treatment to people.
Aluminium is a metal which is produced from bauxite.

Note: *Who* is used for persons, *which* is used for inanimate objects and animals, *where* is used for places.

Complete the following sentences in the same way as the examples above.

a A college _____ students receive higher or professional education.
b A dentist _____ treats people's teeth.
c Steel _____ is produced from iron and carbon. (We can also say that steel is an alloy.)

2 Join pairs of sentences by using relative clauses.

e.g. Bronze is an alloy. It is produced from copper and tin.
Bronze is an alloy *which* is produced from copper and tin.

The sentences in the box overleaf have been mixed up. Join the 8 sentences on the left with the correct ones from the 10 on the right. Use the appropriate relative pronoun.

1 An engineer is a person		a	It produces electricity.
		b	He studies the way in which industry and trade produce and use wealth.
2 A microscope is an instrument		c	He treats the diseases of animals.
3 A generator is a machine		d	It makes distant objects appear nearer and larger.
4 A botanist is a person		e	He designs machines, buildings or public works.
5 A square is a geometric figure		f	It gives information on subjects in alphabetical order.
6 A cucumber is a vegetable		g	He studies plants.
7 An economist is a person		h	It makes very small near objects appear larger.
8 An encyclopaedia is a book		i	It is long and round with a dark green skin and light green watery flesh.
		j	It has four equal sides and four right angles.

3 So far, in the definitions we have looked at, the language construction has been:

Thing to be defined + verb + general class word + 'wh'-word + particular characteristics. e.g. *A botanist is a person who studies plants.*

Three types of mistakes may occur when a short definition is being written:
1 An *example* may be given rather than a definition. An example may, of course, follow a definition but it should not take its place.
2 The general *class*, or the particular *characteristics*, may be omitted from the definition. It will then be incomplete.
3 The word to be defined, or another form of it, may be used in the definition itself. Clearly, if the reader does not already understand the word, he/she will not understand the repeated use of it.

a Study the following definitions. Each one contains one of the mistakes listed above. Analyse the *type* of mistake (1, 2, 3—listed above) that has been made. Write the *number* of the type of mistake in the column provided. The first one has been done as an example.

	DEFINITION	Type of mistake
	An ammeter is used to measure electric current.	2
i	A lecturer is a person who lectures.	
ii	A dictionary is a book like 'Collins Cobuild English Dictionary'.	
iii	A degree is given by a university to a student who has passed the appropriate examinations.	

b Now re-write the definitions above in a more satisfactory way. The first one has been done as an example.

An ammeter is an instrument which is used to measure electric current.

Stage 2
Academic Definitions

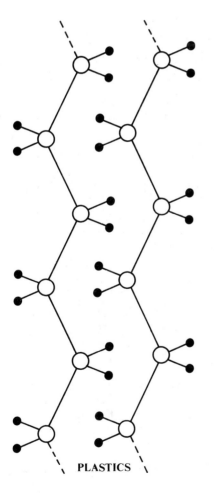

PLASTICS

1 Look at the following definition.

Plastics are compounds made with long chains of carbon atoms.

You will notice that the *wh*-word has been omitted. A definition written in this way uses a *reduced relative clause*. In full the definition would be:

Plastics are compounds *which are* made with long chains of carbon atoms.

Write out the following definitions in full, putting the *wh*-word in the correct place.

1 Plastics are substances moulded into shape when they are heated.
2 A mineral is a structurally homogeneous solid of definite chemical composition formed by the inorganic processes of nature.

Write out the following definitions omitting the *wh*-word so that a *reduced relative clause* is used.

3 Rayons are man-made fibres which are produced from wood.
4 A fossil is an inorganic trace which is buried by natural processes and subsequently permanently preserved.

2a Often subjects, particularly academic subjects, omit the *wh*-word in the following way:

Criminology *is the study of* crime (or illegal acts).
Psychiatry *is the study* and treatment *of* mental illness.
Politics *is the science of* government.
Botany *is the science of* the structure of plants.

Write out definitions of the subjects given below. Use the notes given next to each subject; write in the same style as above.

1 Demography—study—population growth and its structure.
2 Zoology—science—structure, forms and distribution of animals.
3 Biology—science—physical life of animals and plants.

b Academic subjects may be more cautiously defined, thus:

Geography *may be defined as the science of* the earth's surface.
Linguistics *may be defined as the science of* language.

Write out definitions of the following subjects in the same way as above.

1 Sociology—science—nature and growth of society and social behaviour.
2 Theology—study—religious beliefs and theories.
3 Astronomy—science—sun, moon, stars and planets.

c Write a definition of your subject in a similar way to the above.

Stage 3
Extended Definitions

It is possible for academic subjects to be defined more specifically. Normally, this can only be done if more information is given.

1 Look at the following example (*branch* has the meaning of *division*).

Psychology *may be defined as the branch of* biological science *which studies* the phenomena of conscious life and behaviour.

Write out definitions of the following subjects in the same way as above.

1 Criminal psychology—psychology—investigates the psychology of crime and the criminal.
2 Chemistry—science—deals with the composition and behaviour of substances.
3 Social economics—economics—is concerned with the measurement, causes and consequences of social problems.

2a A definition may be extended in order to be more precise and/or to give more information about the subject. Look carefully at the following examples.

Sociology may be defined as the branch of science which studies the development and principles of social organisation. *It is concerned with* group behaviour as distinct from the behaviour of individuals in the group.

Econometrics may be defined as the branch of economics which applies mathematical and statistical techniques to economic problems. *It is concerned with* testing the validity of economic theories and providing the means of making quantitative predictions.

b Now write a definition of your subject in a similar way to the above.

3 Use your dictionary to check definitions. Sometimes it is useful to compare definitions and explanations in two or three dictionaries: they are not always exactly the same, and they often give different examples.

Check the definitions of the following:

a   polytechnic (compared with 'university')
b   standard of living
c   household
d   durable goods
e   consumer
f   perishables

> **Note:**   These words all appear in Unit 11, Stage 3 (page 70).

Structure and Vocabulary Aid

A Frequently used verb tenses for definitions:
    Present Simple (Active *and* Passive)

B Relative clauses are often used to qualify or give extra information.

C Useful verbs:

X   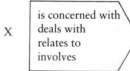   Y

is concerned with
deals with
relates to
involves

Unit 6 Exemplification

The last unit was concerned with definitions. It is often useful in definitions to give examples: this action is known as *exemplification* (or exemplifying).
E.g. (= this is an abbreviation meaning *for example*):

> Linguistics may be defined as the science of language, *for example*, its structure, sound systems, acquisition.

There are different ways of exemplifying, e.g.

> Geology may be defined as the science of the earth's history *as shown by* its crust, rocks, etc.

Geography may be defined as the science of the earth's surface. It is concerned with a number of features, *particularly* physical, climate and produc

(Here *particularly* has the meaning 'more than some others'.)

Exemplification is commonly used throughout academic writing.

Stage 1 Words

top: great tit
bottom: British Army soldier

1 Read the following carefully.

What is Language?

A language is a signalling system which operates with symbolic vocal sounds, and which is used by a group of people for the purposes of communication.

Let us look at this definition in more detail because it is
5 language, more than anything else, that distinguishes man from the rest of the animal world.

Other animals, it is true, communicate with one another by means of cries: for example, many birds utter warning calls at the approach of danger; apes utter different cries, such as
10 expressions of anger, fear and pleasure. But these various means of communication differ in important ways from human language. For instance, animals' cries are not articulate. This means, basically, that they lack structure. They lack, for example, the kind of structure given by the contrast
15 between vowels and consonants. They also lack the kind of structure that enables us to divide a human utterance into words.

We can change an utterance by replacing one word in it by another: a good illustration of this is a soldier who can say,
20 e.g., 'tanks approaching from the north', or he can change one word and say 'aircraft approaching from the north' or 'tanks approaching from the west'; but a bird has a single alarm cry, which means 'danger!'

This is why the number of signals that an animal can make
25 is very limited: the great tit is a case in point; it has about

twenty different calls, whereas in human language the number of possible utterances is infinite. It also explains why animal cries are very general in meaning.

a Read the passage again and draw a ⬚box⬚ around all the words which have the same meaning as the word *example*. Notice how they are used and the punctuation that is used with them.

b Now draw a line under all the examples. e.g.

⬚For example,⬚ many birds utter warning calls at the approach of danger.

2 The following sentences are based upon the information contained in the passage above. Complete the sentences making use of each of the following words (use each only once).

> illustration   for example   a case in point   an example
>   for instance   such as

1 At the approach of danger many birds utter warning calls: this is _____ of animals communicating with each other.
2 Cries, _____ those of anger, fear and pleasure, are uttered by apes.
3 There are important differences between human language and animal communication. _____, animals' cries are not articulate.
4 Animals' cries lack, _____, the kind of structure that enables us to divide a human utterance into words.
5 A good _____ of changing an utterance by substituting one word for another is a soldier who can say 'tanks approaching from the north' or 'tanks approaching from the west'.
6 The number of signals that an animal can make is very limited: the great tit is _____.

Stage 2 Sentences

1 Look at the following:

Language Families

Latin

Portuguese   Spanish   Italian   French   Romanian   etc.

1 There are a number of languages which are descended from Latin: for example, Portuguese and Italian.
This can be expressed another way:

2 There are a number of languages, such as Portuguese and Italian, which are descended from Latin.

a Write two sentences about the following information: one sentence as in 1 above, and then another sentence as in 2.

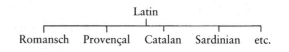

b Now write two sentences about the following, one as in 1 and another as in 2 above.

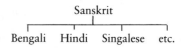

2 Read the following carefully, especially the parts in italics.

There are now over two thousand different languages in the world; an examination of them shows that many of them belong to a group of related languages, and some of these groups are very large, constituting what we can call language families. *An example of such a family is the Semitic group of languages. Examples of members of the family are Arabic and Hebrew.*

Now write out the last two sentences substituting the following (not all the examples need to be listed).

a Germanic—e.g. English, German, Dutch, Swedish, Danish, Norwegian.

b Sino-Tibetan—e.g. Thai, Burmese, Chinese, Tibetan.

Stage 3 Paragraphs

1 Here are some notes on *writing systems*. Read them carefully.

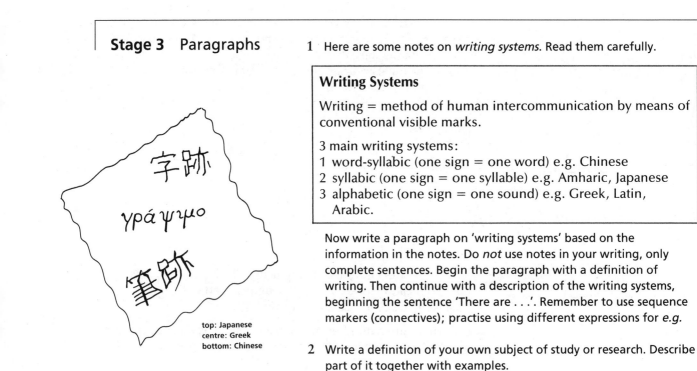

top: Japanese
centre: Greek
bottom: Chinese

Writing Systems

Writing = method of human intercommunication by means of conventional visible marks.

3 main writing systems:
1 word-syllabic (one sign = one word) e.g. Chinese
2 syllabic (one sign = one syllable) e.g. Amharic, Japanese
3 alphabetic (one sign = one sound) e.g. Greek, Latin, Arabic.

Now write a paragraph on 'writing systems' based on the information in the notes. Do *not* use notes in your writing, only complete sentences. Begin the paragraph with a definition of writing. Then continue with a description of the writing systems, beginning the sentence 'There are . . .'. Remember to use sequence markers (connectives); practise using different expressions for *e.g.*

2 Write a definition of your own subject of study or research. Describe part of it together with examples.

**Structure and
Vocabulary Aid**

A Alternatives to the word *examples* are: *cases, instances*.

B Other commonly used verb forms and methods of expression
are:

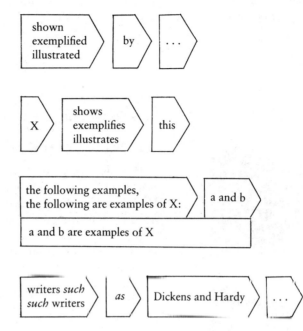

Unit 7   Classification

When we divide something into groups, classes, categories, etc. we are *classifying* those items. The classification is normally made according to a criterion or several criteria (standards or principles on which judgements are based).

Stage 1   Criteria

from top to bottom: a large comprehensive school, a technical college, a primary school, a small traditional grammar school.

1   Read the following carefully.

State Schools In England and Wales

The vast majority of children in Britain (87%) attend state (local authority) schools which provide compulsory education from the age of 5 to 16 years. These schools can be classified according to the age range of the pupils and the type of
5   education provided. Basically, there are two types of school: primary and secondary, although in some areas there are also middle schools. Primary schools cater for children aged 5–11, and secondary schools for ages 11–16 (and in some areas up to 18 years). Primary schools can be sub-divided into infant
10   schools (for ages 5–7) and junior schools (for ages 7–11).

Secondary schools are normally of one type for all abilities, viz. comprehensive schools. More than 90% of children in state schools attend this kind of school. In some areas middle schools exist as an extra level after primary school for children
15   aged 8 or 9 to 12 or 13. Pupils then transfer to senior comprehensive schools. In a small number of areas, pupils may be grouped according to their ability and selected by means of an examination at the age of 11. In these areas, grammar schools cater for those with academic ability and
20   secondary modern schools for those with less academic ability.

When pupils reach the age of 16 there may be three choices open to them. Firstly, they may leave school. Secondly they may stay on at school for two more years if it has a Sixth
25   Form. Thirdly, they may transfer to a Sixth Form College or a Tertiary College.

Now complete the following sentences which are based upon the text above.

a   Schools _____ the pupils' ages and the type of education.

b   There are _____ school: primary and secondary.

c   Primary schools _____ into infant and junior schools.

d   Secondary school pupils _____ their ability.

e   The *criterion* for classifying secondary schools is whether or not there is _____.

2 Below there are seven sentences, labelled **a–g**, which summarise the information in the passage. The sentences are in the wrong order. Put them in the correct order by writing the appropriate letter next to the numbers 1–7.

a Most children go to comprehensive schools.
b There may be three types of school: primary, middle and secondary.
c At the age of sixteen, pupils may stay on at school, or leave and go to a college, or leave school altogether.
d Exceptionally, children may take a selection exam at 11 years and go to either a grammar or a secondary modern school.
e Most children go to state schools.
f If children attend middle schools, they go on to senior comprehensive schools afterwards.
g Primary schools comprise both infant and junior schools.

3a Look at *Diagram 1*. It shows a diagrammatic classification of state schools in England and Wales. If necessary read the text again and then complete *Diagram 1*, writing on the lines provided.

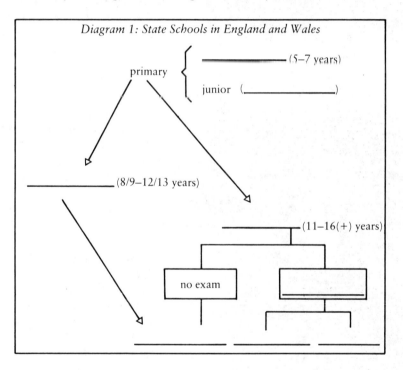

Diagram 1: State Schools in England and Wales

primary
———————— (5–7 years)
junior (————————)
———————— (8/9–12/13 years)
(11–16(+) years)
no exam

b Without looking at the text again, write a brief description of the information contained in *Diagram 1*. Begin your description:

There are two types of school: primary and secondary. Primary schools can be sub-divided, according to age, into . . .

Note: If any help is needed with the language of classification in this exercise, or the following ones, turn to the *Structure and Vocabulary Aid* at the end of this unit (page 46).

4 Try to draw a classification diagram of the education system in your country. When you have completed it, write a brief description of it.

Stage 2 Classifying

a crow

a golden eagle

a sparrow

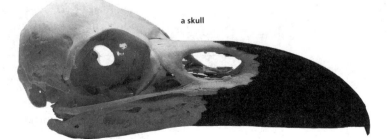

feathers

1   Read the following carefully.

The Classification of Birds

Birds are instantly recognisable creatures. Perhaps it is their ability to fly that causes this. Some people might consider that their shape was the most distinguishing feature. Everyone, however, agrees upon the characteristics that a bird
5   possesses: two wings, feathers, two legs, a toothless bill or beak, warm blood, and it lays eggs.

The modern system of classifying birds is like a pyramid, with the base formed by 8514 different *species*. A convenient definition of species is: an interbreeding group of birds which
10   do not normally mate with other such groups.

The next division above the species is the *genus*, a group of species showing strong similarities. The scientific name of a bird gives the genus first, then the species. Thus, the scientific (Latin) name of the golden eagle is 'Aquila
15   chrysaëtos' (eagle, golden). When there are strong points of similarity between one genus and another, these related genera are grouped together and are said to belong to the same *family*. The names of the 215 families of birds always end in 'idae'. The golden eagle, for instance, is one of the
20   'Falconidae' (falcon family).

Families with broadly similar characteristics are grouped together into 27 *orders*, whose names end in 'iformes'. The golden eagle falls into the order of 'Falconiformes' (falcon-like birds). The largest order is 'Passeriformes' or perching birds.
25   This contains 63 families, and more species than all the rest put together. The feet are designed so that they can grip a perch, with three toes in front and one behind. In addition, all are known as song-birds. Two large families within this order are sparrows, with 155 species, and crows, with 100
30   species.

Finally, all of the orders make up the *class* 'Aves' (birds). This system of classification has enabled scientists to differentiate 8514 species of birds. Placing a bird in the right *family* depends upon a number of features. Among them are
35   external characteristics, such as the shape of the beak and feet, and the colour pattern of the feathers. However, at the level of *order*, the next higher category, distinctions are based on such features as the structure of the skull, the arrangement of the muscles in the legs, and the condition of
40   the young at the time of hatching.

a skull

2   Look at *Diagram 2* (The Classification of Birds). If necessary, read the text again and then complete the table. Parts of it have been filled in already to help you. Note that the centre column should contain examples relating to the bird 'golden eagle' (in English).

Diagram 2: The Classification of Birds

Classification divisions or categories	Example of classification of *Golden Eagle* for each division	Number of the divisions
ORDER	FALCON-LIKE	
	GOLDEN EAGLE	8514

3   From the information in the text:
 a   give a definition of *a bird*
 b   give a definition of *a species*.
 c   give two criteria that are used in assigning birds to the order of *Passeriformes*.
 d   give two examples of families of birds from the order of *Passeriformes*.
 e   list some of the general characteristics of *families* of birds, and then of *orders* of birds.

4a   Write a brief general description of the classification of birds: base your description upon the information contained in *Diagram 2*.
 b   Write in a similar way to the following classification of *vegetables*.

There are six main groups of vegetables, for example, legumes. Each group may be divided into members, such as beans, and each member may be sub-divided into types: Scarlet Runners are an example. Finally, each type may be further subdivided into a number of varieties, e.g. Prizewinner.

Stage 3   Diagrams

1   Look carefully at *Diagram 3* on page 46. It is a tree diagram classification of drinks.
 a   What are the three criteria that are used in the classification?
 b   Write a description of the classification of drinks based upon the information in *Diagram 3*. Begin your description:

Drinks may be classified into two main groups: . . .

Diagram 3: A Classification of Drinks

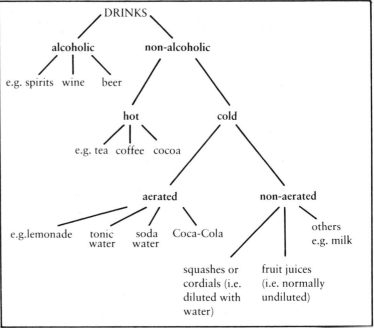

an aerated/gaseous/'fizzy' drink

Now draw a diagram for the subject, or part of it, that you are studying. Write a brief description of the classification diagram, making sure that it is clear what the criteria are. If a classification diagram is not appropriate for your subject, perhaps an organisational diagram (showing hierarchy etc.) would be possible.

Structure and Vocabulary Aid

A

criterion/criteria
basis/bases
features
characteristics

to . . .	*to . . .*	two, etc.	categories	sub-category
classify	sub-classify	several	classes	sub-class
categorise	sub-categorise	a number of	groups	sub-group
group	sub-group	various	types	sub-order
divide into	sub-divide	the following	kinds	sub-division
arrange (in)		main	sorts	
put into		general	species	
fall into		broad	breeds	
place in		orders	orders	
distinguish (between)			divisions	
differentiate (between/from)			families	
			members	

Note: Not all the nouns above are interchangeable: some are restricted to certain disciplines e.g. 'species'—biology, botany, zoology.

X 〉 consists of . . . / comprises . . . 〉 according to 〉 *whether or not . . .* there is X . . . / *whether* there is X *or not . . .*

X may be classified 〉 according to . . . / on the basis of . . . / depending (up)on . . .

The classification is based (up)on . . .

Note the possible sequence:

. . . may be divided . . .
. . . may be sub-divided . . .
. . . may be further sub-divided . . .

B Vocabulary: Schools in England and Wales

1 State: non-fee-paying

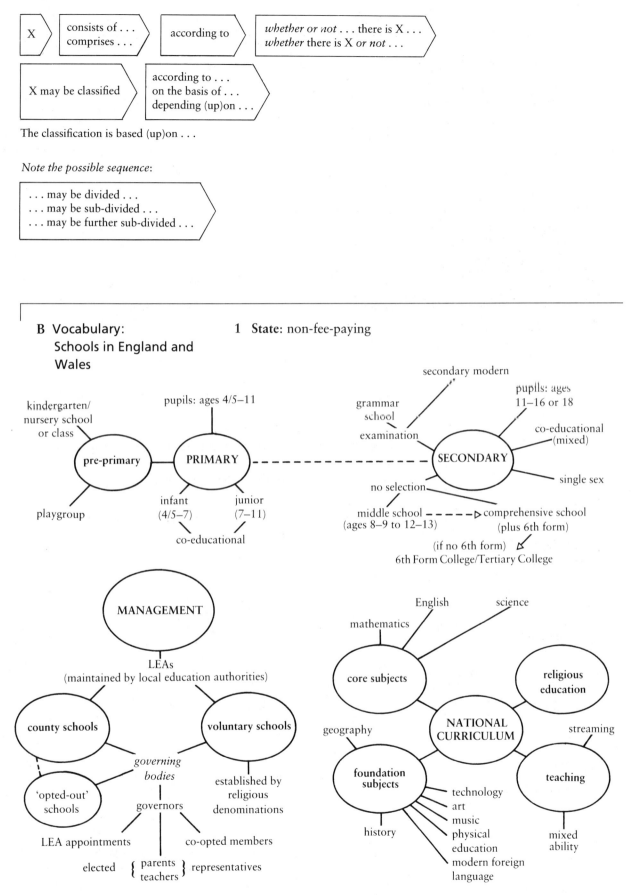

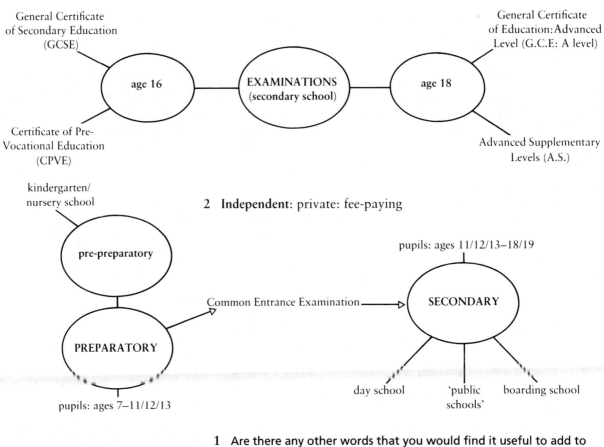

General Certificate
of Secondary Education
(GCSE)

age 16

EXAMINATIONS
(secondary school)

age 18

General Certificate
of Education: Advanced
Level (G.C.E: A level)

Certificate of Pre-
Vocational Education
(CPVE)

Advanced Supplementary
Levels (A.S.)

kindergarten/
nursery school

pre-preparatory

2 **Independent**: private: fee-paying

pupils: ages 11/12/13–18/19

SECONDARY

Common Entrance Examination

PREPARATORY

pupils: ages 7–11/12/13

day school   'public
schools'   boarding school

1 Are there any other words that you would find it useful to add to
   the above lists?
2 Make a similar list for the school system in your country.

Unit 8 Comparison and Contrast

In most academic subjects, and in life generally, we often need to *compare* and *contrast* things. Similarities and differences are often noted when classifying (see the previous unit). The language of comparison and contrast is frequently needed when studying tables and other statistical information. The language forms used in this unit are to be found in *Appendix 7: Comparisons* (page 116).

Stage 1 Comparison

1 Look at Tables 1 and 2.

Table 1: The Longest Rivers in the World

> 1 The Nile (Africa)—4,160 miles (6,695 kilometres)
> 2 The Amazon (South America)—4,080 miles (6,570 kilometres)
> 3 The Mississippi-Missouri (North America)—3,740 miles (6,020 kilometres)
> 4 The Yangtse (Asia, China)—3,430 miles (5,520 kilometres)

Table 2: Temperatures and Rainfall in Beijing, China

Month	J	F	M	A	M	J	J	A	S	O	N	D
Temperature (°C)	−4.7	−1.5	5.0	13.7	19.9	24.5	26.0	24.7	19.8	12.5	3.6	−2.6
Rainfall (cm)	0.2	0.5	0.5	1.5	3.6	7.6	23.9	16.0	6.6	1.5	0.8	0.2

top: the Nile (by satellite)
bottom: the Amazon (aerial view)

Note:

a the first month is January (J), the last is December (D).
b the temperature is measured in Centigrade, and is an average.
c the rainfall is measured in centimetres, and is also an average.

Now complete the following sentences. If necessary, look at *Appendix 7: Comparisons*. Put one or more words in each space.

Table 1:

1 The Nile is _____ the Mississippi–Missouri.
2 The Amazon is _____ long _____ the Nile.
3 The Nile is _____ river in the world.
4 The Mississippi–Missouri is _____ the Amazon.
5 The Yangtse is _____ river in China.

Table 2:

6 In Beijing, January is a _____ month _____ _____ December.
7 July is a _____ month _____ June.
8 There is _____ rain in May _____ in March.

49

9 July has the _____ rain; in other words, July is _____ month.

10 August is _____ warm _____ July.

11 December and January are _____ months.

12 The rainfall in February is _____ in March.

13 April is _____ wet _____ October.

14 The rainfall in November is _____ in May.

15 July is the _____ month, and also _____ month.

2 Look at Table 3.

Table 3: The Highest Mountains in the World

> 1 Everest (Nepal/Tibet)—29,028 feet (8,848 metres)
>
> 2 K2 (Kashmir/Sinkiang)—28,250 feet (8,611 metres)
>
> 3 Kangchenjunga (Nepal/Sikkim)—28,168 feet (8,586 metres)
>
> 4 Makalu (Nepal/Tibet)—27,805 feet (8,475 metres)
>
> 5 Dhaulagiri (Nepal)—26,810 feet (8,172 metres)

Note: All the mountains above are in the Himalayas.

Now write at least three sentences comparing the mountains.

3 Turn back to Unit 2 Stage 2 (page 15). Look at the information in the table about Manchester University students. Write several sentences comparing the information: e.g. More students write essays than any other type of writing.

Stage 2
Extended Comparison

1 Read the following carefully.

Several years ago, some research was conducted at Manchester University into the amount of time that overseas postgraduate students spent listening to spoken English and speaking English. Sixty students co-operated by completing questionnaires.

It was found that an average of 22¾ hours *per week* were spent listening to English and only 6¼ hours speaking English to English people. An analysis of the time spent listening to English showed that lectures accounted for 5 hours and seminars 2 hours. An estimated 2½ hours were spent in serious discussion while 2 hours were devoted to everyday small-talk. Watching television accounted for 5¼ hours and listening to the radio 4½ hours. Going to the cinema or theatre only accounted for an average of ¾ hour per week.

The following sentences are based upon the information contained in the text above. Complete the sentences by choosing from the list of words and phrases below: use each word once only. Make sure that you keep the *same meaning* in the sentences as in the text.

Choose from these words: biggest; as much . . . as; more . . . than (*twice*); least; most; not so many . . . as; as many . . . as; the same . . . as; greater . . . than.

a The students spent considerably _____ time listening to English _____ speaking it.

b A _____ amount of time was spent in lectures _____ in seminars.

c Nearly _____ hours were spent listening to the radio _____ watching television.

d The _____ popular way of listening to English was by watching TV.

e _____ number of hours was spent in everyday small-talk _____ in taking part in seminars.

f The _____ popular way of listening to English was by going to the cinema.

g _____ hours were spent in serious discussion _____ _____ in watching television.

h Nearly _____ time was spent in watching television _____ in speaking English

i _____ time was spent in serious discussion _____ _____ in everyday small-talk.

j The _____ surprise in the survey was the small number of hours spent speaking English to English people.

2 You have just received a letter from a friend, or acquaintance, asking for some information about English dictionaries and asking you to recommend a suitable one to help him/her learn English. Look at *Table 4: English Dictionaries*, then on the basis of that information write a letter recommending one of the dictionaries. Give reasons for your choice. Look at the *Structure and Vocabulary Aid* at the end of this unit (page 54) and at the *Notes* in the *Key* if you need some help with the letter.

Table 4: English Learners' Dictionaries

feature \ dictionary	Collins COBUILD English Language Dictionary	Collins COBUILD Essential English Dictionary	Longman Active Study Dictionary	Longman Dictionary of Contemporary English	Oxford Advanced Learner's Dictionary	Oxford Student's Dictionary of Current English
words and phrases	70,000	45,000	38,000	56,000	57,000	35,000
examples	90,000	50,000	55,000	75,000	81,500	35,000 approx.
illustrations	—	75	26	500	1,800	—
appendices	—	—	—	8	11	4
pages	1,703	948	710	1,258	1,580	774
page size	17 × 24.5 cm.	15.5 × 22 cm.	12.5 × 19.5 cm.	14 × 21.5 cm.	13.5 × 21.5 cm.	11.5 × 18.5 cm.
price (1989): hardback / paperback	£12.95 / £ 7.95	£6.25 / £4.95	— / £4.50	£9.75 / £6.95	£10.50 / £ 6.95	£4.50
level	advanced	intermediate	intermediate	advanced	advanced	intermediate

Stage 3
Similarities and Differences

Look carefully at the information below.

Table 5: Nordic Countries (1988)

information country	DENMARK	FINLAND	NORWAY	SWEDEN
Population	5,116,273	4,926,200	4,200,000	8,400,000
Area: square kilometres	43,092	337,032	323,878	450,000
Density: per sq. km.	118.7	14.6	13.0	18.7
Temperature (Centigrade) summer: average winter: average	16.6°C −0.4°C	17°C −9°C	17°C −4°C	18°C −2°C
Forest area	10%	65%	18%	55%
Agricultural area	70%	17%	3%	10%
Constitution	constitutional monarchy	republic	constitutional monarchy	constitutional monarchy
Religion	Christianity: Lutheran	Christianity: Lutheran	Christianity: Lutheran	Christianity: Lutheran
Language	Danish	Finnish (minority: Swedish)	Norwegian	Swedish

1   **Similarities:** there are a number of language constructions that express similarity apart from those listed in *Appendix 7: Comparisons* (section 2), on page 117.

a   Look at the following examples based on the table above.

1   *Both* Denmark *and* Norway have a constitutional monarchy.
2   Denmark *and* Norway are *similar* (or: *alike*) *in that they both* have a constitutional monarchy.
3   Sweden is *similar* to Norway *in that* it has a small agricultural area.
4   Sweden is *similar* to Norway *in* its constitution.
5   Denmark *and* Sweden *both* have the *same kind of* constitution.
6   Denmark, *like* Finland, has a population of about 5 million.

Still more sentences may be composed by using the connectives listed in *Appendix 8: Connectives* (section 1a: Addition page 118), e.g. Finland is very cold in winter; so, *too*, is Norway.

b   Now write one sentence similar to each of the previous six types, basing your information on *Table 5*.

2   **Differences:** see *Appendix 7: Comparisons* (section 2) and *Appendix 8: Connectives* (section i: Contrast; section j: Concession page 121).

a   Look at the following examples based on *Table 5*.

1   Norway and Sweden are *dissimilar in that* Norway has a *much* small*er* population *than* Sweden.

2 Denmark is *different from* (or: *unlike*) Finland *in that* it has a constitutional monarchy (. . . *whereas* Finland is a republic).
3 *With regard to* population, Sweden is bigg*er than* Norway.
4 Denmark has a constitutional monarchy, *whereas* (or: *while*) Finland is a republic.
5 *Whereas* Finland is a republic, Norway has a constitutional monarchy.
6 Denmark has *the* small*est* land area; *however*, it has *the* larg*est* percentage agricultural area.
7 *Although* Denmark has *the* small*est* land area, it has *the* larg*est* percentage agricultural area.
8 (*On the one hand*,) Denmark has *the* small*est* land area; *on the other hand*, it has *the* larg*est* percentage agricultural area.
9 *The main difference* / *One of the differences between* Finland *and* Sweden *is that* Finland is a republic, *whereas* Sweden has a constitutional monarchy.

b Now write one sentence similar to each of the above nine types, basing your information on *Table 5*.

3 Turn to Unit 3, Stage 2 (page 22). Look at the table of information about Iceland beneath the map. Write a paragraph to compare and contrast Iceland with Denmark in terms of area, population, density and agricultural area.

4 Compare and contrast *your* country with *one* of the Nordic countries in *Table 5*. It is not necessary to refer to all the items. If you do not know some of the details for your country, give a rough estimation; but try to find out by looking in appropriate reference books. If necessary, look at the *Structure and Vocabulary Aid* in this unit, below and in Unit 3 (page 23) to help you.

Structure and Vocabulary Aid

A Qualification of Comparison.

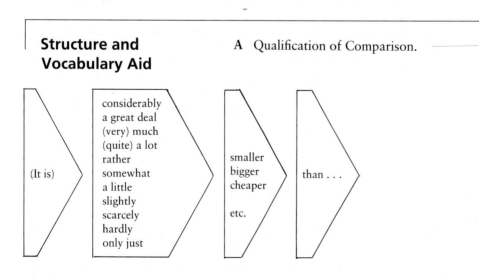

(It is)

considerably
a great deal
(very) much
(quite) a lot
rather
somewhat
a little
slightly
scarcely
hardly
only just

smaller
bigger
cheaper

etc.

than . . .

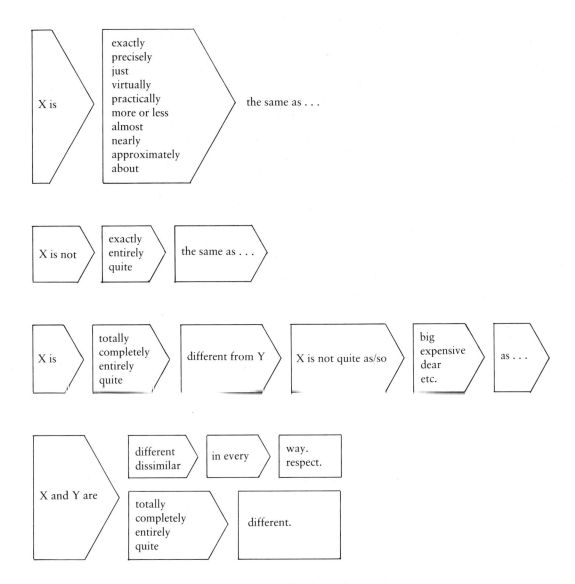

B Cardinal numbers.

When writing figures involving *thousands*, a space is used to separate the thousands if there are 5 or more digits:

e.g. 10 000   100 000   1 000 000   *but* 1000

Alternatively a comma may be used to separate the thousands:

e.g. 1,000   10,000   100,000   1,000,000

A point is used in writing decimal fractions: e.g. 1293.75

C *Ordinal* numbers are often written in abbreviated form:

1st − first
2nd − second
3rd − third
4th − fourth
5th − fifth

'th' is used after all numbers except those ending in 1, 2, or 3.

Unit 9 Cause and Effect

In academic writing, events or actions are frequently linked with their *cause* and *effect*. Look at the following diagram which summarises this relationship.

back in time or sequence cause reason purpose	← event situation action idea problem →	forward in time or sequence effect consequence result solution

Now look at these examples of the cause and effect relationship.

connective

Heat	causes	iron to expand.
Prices rose.	As a result	fewer goods were sold.

Any marks on the leaves are probably	due to	the same virus.

The cause is in a box; the effect is underlined.

There are a large number of ways to express the relationship shown in the diagram on the left. You will need to look at *Appendix 8: Connectives* (section e: Result, page 120) and especially the *Structure and Vocabulary Aid* at the end of this unit (page 60).

Sometimes the cause will be named before the effect; sometimes the effect will be named first. e.g.

1) **X causes**   **Y (active verb)**
      ↑   ↑
    cause   **effect**

2) **Y is caused by**   **X (passive verb)**
      ↑   ↑
    effect   **cause**

Stage 1
Connectives and Markers

Look carefully at the *Structure and Vocabulary Aid* at the end of this unit (page 60), then do the following exercises.

1   The parts of the sentences below have been mixed up. Join the 6 parts on the left with the correct parts from the 9 on the right.

1 There is acid in that bottle: *therefore* . . .	a the road was icy.
2 The *effect* of the fluctuation in temperature . . .	b he was unsuccessful.
3 Bad labour relations *caused* . . .	c prolonged illness
4 The accident occurred *because of* . . .	d it must be handled very carefully.
5 He passed his examination *because* . . .	e careful storage.
6 Delayed treatment often *results in* . . .	f the icy road conditions.
	g the strike.
	h he worked hard.
	i was to kill the laboratory specimens.

2 Making use of the information in the correct answers from the previous exercise complete the following sentences. Inside the box write the appropriate connective or verb marker (see the *Structure and Vocabulary Aid*). The first one has been done as an example.

e.g. Icy road conditions [caused] the accident _____ .

a [_____] he worked hard _____ .

b Prolonged illness is often [_____] _____ .

c The strike was [_____] _____ .

d The laboratory specimens were killed [_____] _____ .

e That bottle must be handled very carefully [_____] _____ .

Stage 2
Identifying Relationships

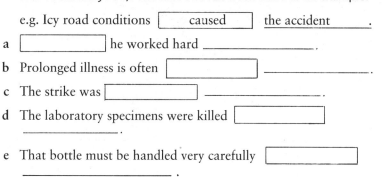

top: glacier
centre: spruce trees
bottom: silver birch

1 Read the following carefully.

Climate

For the last hundred years the climate has been growing much warmer. This has had a number of different effects. Since the beginning of the 20th Century, glaciers have been melting very rapidly. For example, the Muir Glacier in Alaska
5 has retreated 2 miles in 10 years. Secondly, rising temperatures have been causing the snowline to retreat on mountains all over the world. In Peru, for example, it has risen as much as 2700 feet in 60 years.

   As a result of this, vegetation has also been changing. In
10 Canada, the agricultural cropline has shifted 50 to 100 miles northward. In the same way cool-climate trees like birches and spruce have been dying over large areas of Eastern Canada. In Sweden the treeline has moved up the mountains by as much as 65 feet since 1930.

15   The distribution of wildlife has also been affected, many European animals moving northwards into Scandinavia. Since 1918, 25 new species of birds have been seen in Greenland, and in the United States birds have moved their nests to the north.

20   Finally, the sea has been rising at a rapidly increasing rate, largely due, as was mentioned above, to the melting of glaciers. In the last 18 years it has risen by about 6 inches, which is about four times the average rate of rise over the last 9000 years.

Now look at the following cause and effect table. From the text above copy into the table where necessary the *causes* and *effects* mentioned; also write in the central column, the appropriate connective or marker of the cause/effect relationship. Where an example (e.g.) is asked for, only write the first one if more than one is given in the text. The first section has been done as an example.

Table 1: Climate

Cause	Connective or Marker	Effect
The climate has been growing much warmer	(different) effects	1 glaciers have been melting very rapidly, e.g. the Muir Glacier in Alaska has retreated 2 miles in 10 years
		2 e.g.
		3 e.g.
		4 e.g.
		5 e.g.

2   Look at *Table 2* carefully. Then do the exercise which follows.

Table 2: Accidents in a large British city (1987)

	Main accident causes	number of accidents 1987	percentage rise (+)/fall (−) compared with 1986
1	Drivers turning right without due care	593	+12%
2	Pedestrians crossing roads carelessly	402	+ 7%
3	Drivers failing to give a signal	231	− 3%
4	Drivers losing control of vehicles	312	+40%
5	Drivers improperly overtaking other vehicles	173	−10%
6	Drivers misjudging distances	96	−20%

Complete the following description of the information above. In the spaces write a suitable cause-effect *connective*.

Firstly, turning right without due care (1) _____ 593 accidents in 1987. Secondly, (2) _____ pedestrians crossed roads carelessly, 402 accidents occurred. Next, although there was a 3% decrease in drivers failing to give a signal, nevertheless there were still 231 accidents (3) _____

_____ this. In 1987, 40% more drivers than in 1986 lost control of vehicles. (4) _____ there were 312 accidents. In fifth place came drivers improperly overtaking other vehicles: these (5) _____ 173 accidents. Finally, there was a 20% fall in drivers misjudging distances; however, they were still the (6) _____ 96 accidents.

3 Now write a description of *Table 3* in a similar way to the previous exercise. Practise using different connectives but take care to use the correct construction.

Table 3: Accidents in a large British city (1989)

	Main accident causes	number of accidents 1989	percentage rise (+)/fall (−) compared with 1988
1	Drivers travelling too close to other vehicles	347	+ 7%
2	Drivers driving under the influence of alcohol	304	+10%
3	Drivers reversing negligently	169	− 8%
4	Pedestrians crossing roads in dangerous places	113	− 5%
5	Drivers travelling too quickly in bad weather conditions	190	+12%

Stage 3
Constructing Paragraphs

1 Look at the diagram below relating to poverty.

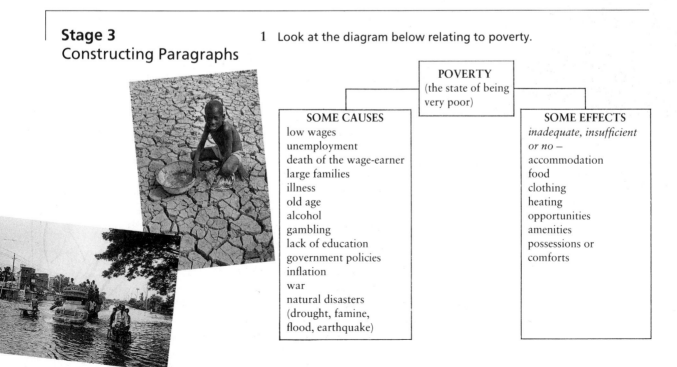

POVERTY
(the state of being very poor)

SOME CAUSES
low wages
unemployment
death of the wage-earner
large families
illness
old age
alcohol
gambling
lack of education
government policies
inflation
war
natural disasters
(drought, famine,
flood, earthquake)

SOME EFFECTS
inadequate, insufficient or no –
accommodation
food
clothing
heating
opportunities
amenities
possessions or
comforts

Now write one or two paragraphs describing some of the causes and effects of poverty in Britain or another industrialised country that you know of. In your description include a definition of poverty.

Note: Causes can have multiple effects, and there can be a circular relationship between cause and effect e.g. unemployment → very little money → few opportunities or amenities → alcohol → illness . . . ?

2 Describe poverty in your country—its main causes and effects. (Who are the poor? Where do they live? Why are they poor? What is the effect on them?)

3 Briefly describe the cause-effect relationship of part of your own specialist subject or of some aspect of studies which you are familiar with.

Structure and Vocabulary Aid

Look carefully at the connectives or markers of cause-effect relationships shown below. Notice particularly how they are used in a sentence construction.

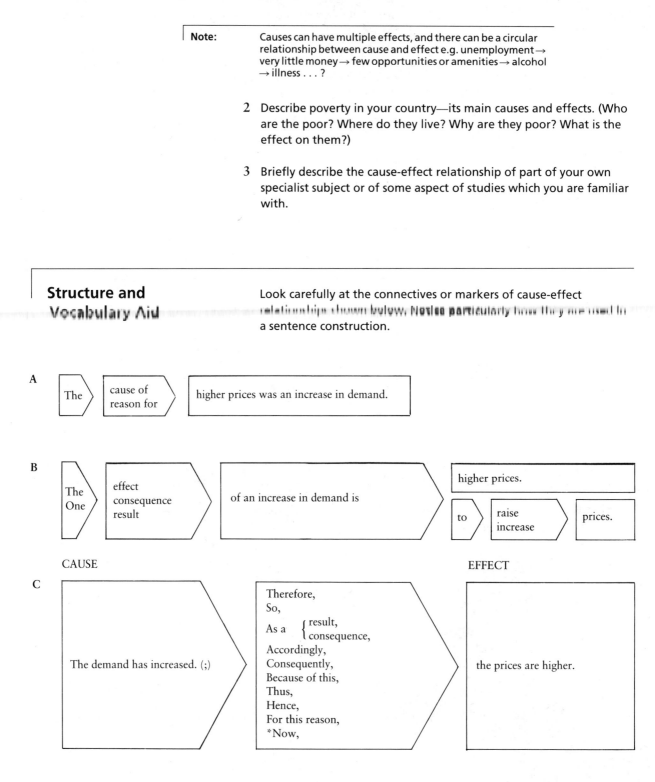

A

The > cause of / reason for > higher prices was an increase in demand.

B

The / One > effect / consequence / result > of an increase in demand is > higher prices. / to > raise / increase > prices.

CAUSE   EFFECT

C

The demand has increased. (;) > Therefore, / So, / As a { result, / consequence, / Accordingly, / Consequently, / Because of this, / Thus, / Hence, / For this reason, / *Now, > the prices are higher.

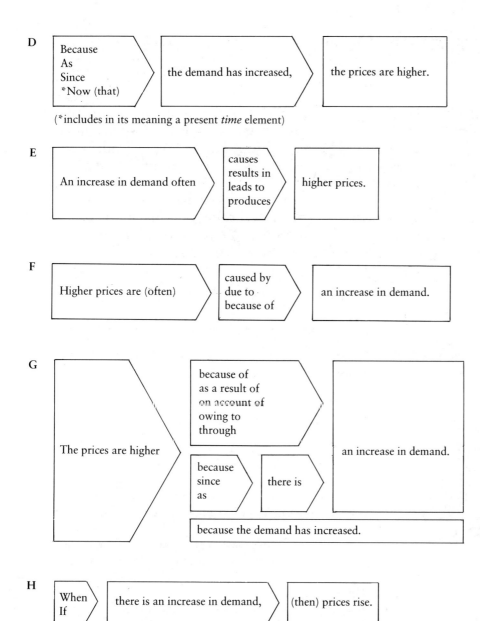

D

Because / As / Since / *Now (that) ⟩ the demand has increased, ⟩ the prices are higher.

(*includes in its meaning a present *time* element)

E

An increase in demand often ⟩ causes / results in / leads to / produces ⟩ higher prices.

F

Higher prices are (often) ⟩ caused by / due to / because of ⟩ an increase in demand.

G

The prices are higher ⟩ because of / as a result of / on account of / owing to / through ⟩ an increase in demand.

because / since / as ⟩ there is ⟩

because the demand has increased.

H

When / If ⟩ there is an increase in demand, ⟩ (then) prices rise.

Unit 10 Generalisation, Qualification and Certainty

In some academic writing it will be necessary simply to give and describe factual information (similar to that in Units 2 and 3). Often, however, it is necessary to make general comments or to generalise about the information. The *generalisations* can be made more precise by qualifying them. When we make a *qualification* we may be giving our own opinion or interpreting the information: this will be examined in more detail in the next unit. Additionally, in academic writing, we often need to be careful about any claims that we make. Such 'cautious' language is looked at in Stage 2. For exercises throughout this unit it will be necessary to refer to the *Structure and Vocabulary Aid* (page 66).

Stage 1   Generalisation

a Read the following paragraph. It is a straightforward description of factual information.

A Survey of Unemployment
A recent survey of people out of work analysed the type of worker who is unemployed. Out of the one million registered as unemployed, one in five were women. 60% of men who were unemployed were to be found in services and engineering. There was a 1 in 8 chance of being unemployed in the construction industry. 1 in 20 were unemployed in industries such as metal goods and textiles.

b Now compare it with the following paragraph. Notice the figures have been changed to generalisations. Underline the changes.

A Survey of Unemployment
A recent survey of people out of work analysed the type of worker who is unemployed. Out of all those registered as unemployed a minority were women. The majority of men who were unemployed were to be found in services and engineering. The chance of being unemployed was also possible in the construction industry. There was a little unemployment in industries such as metal goods and textiles.

Now read the following paragraphs. A number of generalisations have been made which involve qualifying statements.

If somebody was unemployed from engineering, mining or chemicals, he could usually find another job. However, an unemployed person from agriculture or construction seldom found a job again. Job chances were generally much better for manual workers than for office workers.

Most of the unemployed had been without jobs for more than two months. A number had been unemployed for more than a year. Undoubtedly the longer a person is out of work, the more likely it is that he will not find another job. In addition, job prospects are definitely worse for older workers.

With the help of the *Structure and Vocabulary Aid* (page 66), identify the qualifications of *quantity*, *frequency* and *probability* in the three paragraphs above, and write them in the table below. The first ones have been done as examples.

Quantity	Frequency	Probability
all	usually	possible

Stage 2   Qualification

1   Look at the following information which relates to a British university. It shows some of the forms that overseas students completed during their first few weeks in Britain last year.

(% = percentage of students who completed that form)

%	Form
100	University Registration
95	University Library Membership Application
80	National Health Service Registration
56	International Student Identity Card Application
35	Accommodation Office Application
3	Magazine Subscription

Note: Altogether 16 different forms were filled in.

a   Write a paragraph describing the information in the table above. Use quantity qualifications instead of percentage figures. Begin 'Last year all overseas students completed University Registration forms . . .'

b   Making use of the information in the table make generalised *predictive statements* about students coming to the university next year and form-filling. Make use of probability expressions in order to do this, as in the example:

It is certain that (all) students will need to complete a University Registration form.

2   Recently science students were asked if they had difficulty in obtaining their course books from libraries. The diagram indicates their responses.

Changing the percentage figures to *quantity qualifications* describe the information, e.g.

A *few* students were *never* able to obtain their course books from libraries.

55%
sometimes

25%
often

10%
rarely

5%
never

5%
always

(students) %

Stage 3 Certainty

A feature of written academic English is the need to be careful or cautious. Thus, unless there is evidence which indicates 100% certainty, statements or conclusions are normally qualified in some way to make them less definite (therefore words like *all*, *always*, *never* are usually avoided). The purpose is to be accurate and not to make false claims, or claims that may be challenged by others. In other words, allowance should be made for other possible points of view. There are two basic ways of doing this: a) through words from the lists in the *Scale of Qualification* (page 66), especially the *Probability* list and sometimes the *Frequency* list; and b) through *Impersonal verb phrases* that do not declare the writer's own attitude (see *Structure and Vocabulary Aid*, page 67).

1 In the sentences below there are a number of examples of cautious language. Underline the appropriate words. If necessary refer to the *Structure and Vocabulary Aid* (page 67).

Adjusting to higher education

Other new students may refer to feelings of bewilderment because of the differences in size between school and a large university or polytechnic. . . . The sheer variety of possible activities can be confusing. Students who have
5 chosen to cater for themselves may, at first, have difficulty in finding time for shopping and housekeeping. . . . To these domestic problems may be added financial difficulties when grants fail to arrive, often in the case of foreign students who have no family at hand to assist them.
10 Discussion with students in various university departments suggests that some are not so fortunate. . . . Failure to specify and to communicate aims and objectives may also have long-term consequences. . . . Initially practice can be offered in reading, taking notes from lectures or books and, perhaps, in
15 writing brief reports or paragraphs. . . . Skill in skimming articles to select important or relevant points, and use of the index to look up a topic in a number of books, may also need practice. Science students, in particular, tend to grow accustomed to careful, sequential reading through a text and
20 may need reminding that there are other ways of reading and using books. . . . Students' skills in writing often differ widely on entry. Problems most frequently arise with those who seem hardly literate initially. . . .
  The problems of adjusting to life at university, polytechnic
25 or college of higher education can be more acute for mature students, but it does not follow that this will necessarily be the case. . . . Nonetheless, speaking in broad terms it is possible to discern some similarities within groups of mature students that suggest implications for teaching and learning in
30 higher education. It appears, for example, from various studies that there are three main reasons why adults take up full-time study: (1) to make a change in their career; (2) to obtain a job qualification—for such reasons as job promotion; (3) to seek personal and intellectual development.
35 The difficulties facing adult learners can, for convenience,

be categorised into three kinds—social, psychological and physiological. . . . But for others such problems do not seem to arise. . . .

(Extracts from 'Teaching and Learning in Higher Education' by Ruth Beard and James Hartley.)

2 Look carefully at the information in the table below. It lists the language difficulties of overseas students studying in Britain. It compares their problems on arrival with their problems six months later.

English language problems of overseas students in Britain

Language problems	Students: percentage	
	on arrival	6 months later
understanding spoken English	66%	28%
speaking	52%	42%
writing	15%	32%
reading	3%	2%

Note:
a the percentage figures indicate the percentage of students having that particular language problem
b the percentage figures total more than 100% because some students listed more than one problem.

Now read the paragraph below which comments on some of the information.

On arrival in Britain the biggest language problem for overseas students is understanding spoken English. It would seem that the main reasons for this are difficulties in understanding local accents and the speed of speaking of British people. Six months later the problem has declined into third place. It is generally agreed that the main reasons for this are . . .

a Try to complete this sentence adding some possible reasons.
b Write three more paragraphs to describe the remainder of the information. Make use of the *Impersonal verb phrases* in the *Structure and Vocabulary Aid* (page 67) to indicate that cautious conclusions are being reached.

Some possible reasons to account for the difficulties (not the improvements) are listed below. No doubt you can add others!

Difficulties: local accent, speed of speaking, lack of fluency, limited vocabulary, lack of practice, poor teaching, lack of opportunity, poor pronunciation, slow reading speed, literal translation, poor grammar.

Structure and Vocabulary Aid

A Scale of Qualification

percentage guide	QUANTITY	FREQUENCY	PROBABILITY	
			Adverbs/adjectives	Verbs
100%	all/every/each most a majority (of) many/much a lot (of) enough some a number (of) several a minority (of) a few/a little few/little	always usual(ly) normal(ly) general(ly) on the whole regular(ly) often frequent(ly) sometimes occasional(ly) rare(ly) seldom hardly ever scarcely ever	certain(ly) definite(ly) undoubtedly clearly presumably probably/probable likely conceivably possibly/possible perhaps maybe uncertain unlikely	will is/are must/have to should would ought to may might can could will is/are can could } + not
0%	no/none/not any	never		

If you are uncertain if a word is *quantity* or *frequency* you can normally check by seeing if it can be used to answer the following questions:

Quantity: How many? How much?
Frequency: How often?

Some of the probability qualifications can be further qualified, e.g.

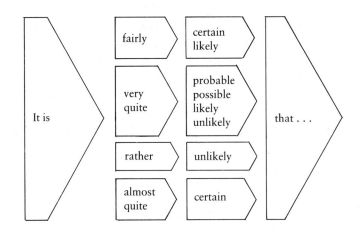

Sometimes generalisations may be introduced or qualified in the following way:

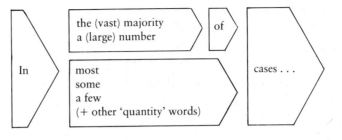

In │ the (vast) majority / a (large) number │ of │ most / some / a few / (+ other 'quantity' words) │ cases . . .

B Impersonal verb phrases often associated with conclusions:

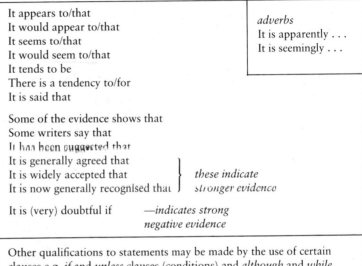

It appears to/that
It would appear to/that
It seems to/that
It would seem to/that
It tends to be
There is a tendency to/for
It is said that

adverbs
It is apparently . . .
It is seemingly . . .

Some of the evidence shows that
Some writers say that
It has been suggested that
It is generally agreed that
It is widely accepted that   } *these indicate*
It is now generally recognised that } *stronger evidence*

It is (very) doubtful if   —*indicates strong negative evidence*

Other qualifications to statements may be made by the use of certain clauses e.g. *if* and *unless* clauses (conditions) and *although* and *while* clauses (concession).

The writer's own attitude can be introduced by, for example:

I think/believe/agree/doubt . . .

(See Unit 12: *Structure and Vocabulary Aid*, page 76)

Unit 11 Interpretation of Data

Unit 10 looked at ways in which we can make generalised statements about information. This unit looks at ways in which we can comment on significant features in diagrammatic information. Discussion of important features and conclusions that can be drawn from this information is covered in Units 12 and 13.

For exercises throughout this unit it will be necessary to refer to the *Structure and Vocabulary Aid* at the end of the unit (page 72). Comparisons and contrasts will frequently be made: you may need to refer to the *Structure and Vocabulary Aid* at the end of Unit 8 (page 54), and to *Appendix 7: Comparisons* (page 116).

Stage 1 Charts

1 Look at the following chart carefully.

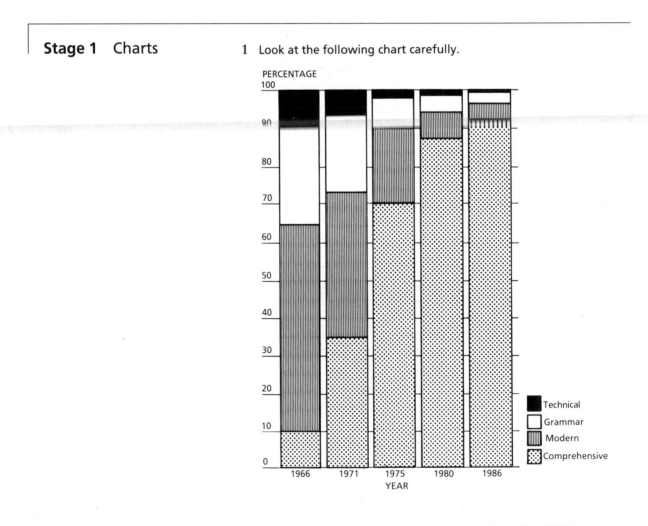

Chart 1: Pupils in state secondary schools in England and Wales

Although the information contained in diagrams etc. is normally clear it usually requires some written comment. Not *all* the information should be described. It is usual to introduce the information with a general comment and then describe or comment on the most *significant* or *important* information.

2 Now read the following.

Introduction
Chart 1 (*a histogram*) shows the percentage of pupils in state secondary schools in England and Wales. The vertical axis shows the percentage of pupils in the different types of secondary school. The horizontal axis compares five years: 1966, 1971, 1975, 1980 and 1986.

Comment
As can be seen from the chart, a larger percentage of secondary school pupils were at comprehensive schools than at any other kind of school in 1986. In fact, comprehensive schools accounted for as much as 92% of the pupils. On the other hand, grammar schools and secondary modern schools together accounted for only 7% of the total.

Note:	a '*in fact*' elaborates, or expands, the previous piece of information.
	b '*as much as*' and '*only*' draw attention to significant items.

3 Comment on the percentage of pupils at secondary modern schools in 1966. Base your comment on the information contained in *Chart 1*. Write in a similar way to the comment above. Draw attention to what is significant. See *Notes on the Exercises* at the back of the book (page 138) for precise figures.

4 Comment on the percentage of pupils at grammar schools and comprehensive schools in 1986 compared with 1966.

Stage 2 Graphs

1 Look at the following graph carefully.

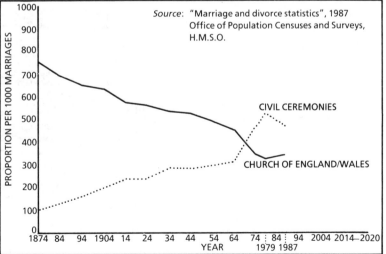

Source: "Marriage and divorce statistics", 1987 Office of Population Censuses and Surveys, H.M.S.O.

Graph 1: Marriages in England and Wales

The graph shows the manner of solemnisation per 1000 marriages at ten-year intervals. Information is given for Church of England/Wales weddings and civil ceremonies. Roman Catholic and other denominational weddings are excluded.

top: a traditional church wedding
bottom: a registry office (civil) wedding

2 Comment on the information in Graph 1. Before you write, look at the *Structure and Vocabulary Aid* at the end of this unit (page 72) and the *Notes on the Exercises* (page 138).

3 Estimate the proportion per 1000 marriages of Church of England weddings and civil ceremonies for the year 2020. Base your prediction on the trend shown in the graph.

Stage 3
Diagrams and Tables

1 One way in which to measure the improvement in the standard of living of a country, over a period of time, is to compare the percentage of people who own, or have access to, certain products that improve the way of life (e.g. make life easier, more comfortable, more enjoyable etc.).

Comment on the significant items and trend(s) shown in the following diagram for the products listed for Britain—cars, central heating, washing machines, refrigerators (or fridges) and fridge-freezers, televisions and telephones.
(Can you give a satisfactory definition of: standard of living; household, durable goods?)

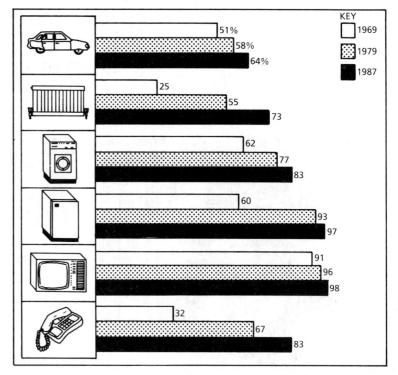

Diagram 1: Percentage of households with certain durable goods (G.B.)

2a Which other items would you include in the list for Britain for the purpose of comparing living standards over a period of time?

b Make a list of items suitable for your country to compare the standard of living 20 or 30 years ago with today. It is not necessary to give figures. Discuss with other students your choice of items. What differences are there? Why?

3 The following diagram (often called a *pie chart*) gives information about family spending in Britain.

Look at the information and then write generalised comments that draw attention to the most significant items.

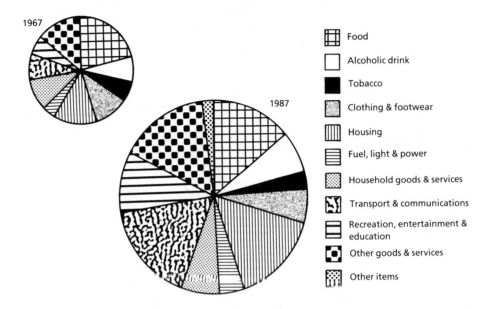

Diagram 2: Average weekly expenditure per family in G.B. (1987)

4 Draw a similar diagram of family spending for your own country, or for your family (exact figures are not needed). Briefly comment on the most significant items.

5 Comment on the trend(s) shown in the following table of family expenditure in Britain. Notice that the data for 1987 are shown in the pie chart above.

Table 1: Average family expenditure in Britain (%)

ITEM	1967	1977	1987
Food	21	19	13
Alcoholic drink	7	7	7
Tobacco	6	4	3
Clothing and footwear	9	8	7
Housing	12	14	15
Fuel, light and power	5	5	4
Household goods and services	10	7	6.5
Transport and communications	9	14	17
Recreation, entertainment and education	7	9	9
Other goods and services	14	12	16
Other items	–	1	2.5

Structure and Vocabulary Aid

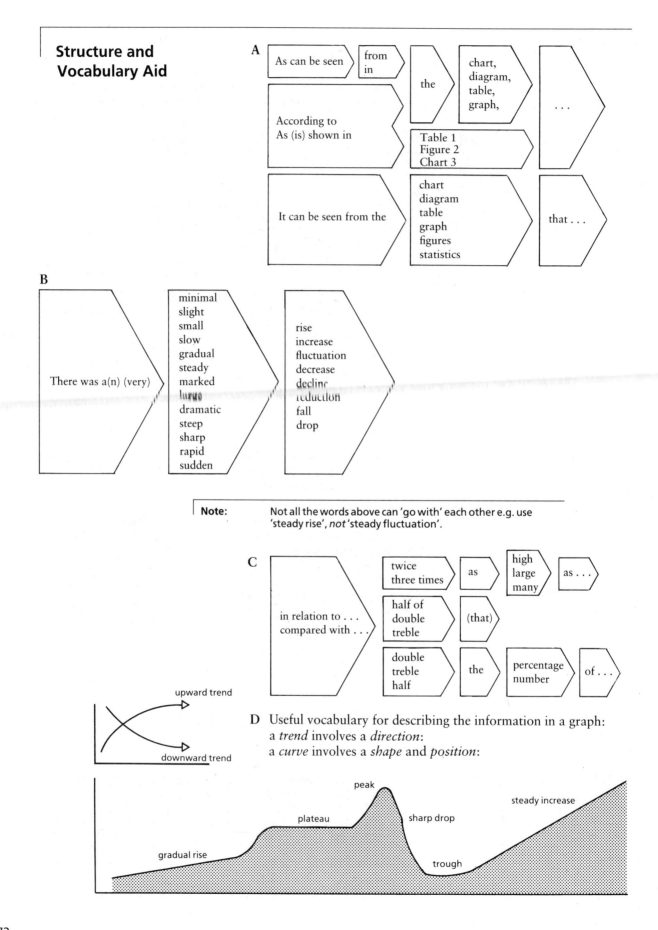

A

As can be seen ▸ from / in ▸ the ▸ chart, diagram, table, graph, ▸ . . .

According to / As (is) shown in ▸ Table 1 / Figure 2 / Chart 3 ▸ . . .

It can be seen from the ▸ chart / diagram / table / graph / figures / statistics ▸ that . . .

B

There was a(n) (very) ▸ minimal / slight / small / slow / gradual / steady / marked / large / dramatic / steep / sharp / rapid / sudden ▸ rise / increase / fluctuation / decrease / decline / reduction / fall / drop

Note: Not all the words above can 'go with' each other e.g. use 'steady rise', *not* 'steady fluctuation'.

C

in relation to . . . / compared with . . . ▸ twice / three times ▸ as ▸ high / large / many ▸ as . . .

half of / double / treble ▸ (that)

double / treble / half ▸ the ▸ percentage / number ▸ of . . .

D Useful vocabulary for describing the information in a graph:
a *trend* involves a *direction*:
a *curve* involves a *shape* and *position*:

upward trend

downward trend

gradual rise · plateau · peak · sharp drop · trough · steady increase

72

Unit 12 Discussion

So far in these units we have practised parts of the language that are useful for particular purposes. In Units 12 and 13 we shall practise putting together a number of the language functions in order to express our ideas. In developing an *argument* or discussion we need to express our opinion or views, and then we need to *conclude*. We shall look at conclusions in Unit 13.

When we discuss or argue in academic writing, we normally need to present a balanced view. We often look at what other people have already said on the same subject or we look at other ideas. We probably look at the *advantages* and *disadvantages* of a particular idea or proposal or action; we look at the arguments *for* (or *in favour*) and *against*.

Then we try to evaluate the different opinions, comparing and contrasting, and eventually give our own opinion or views (see the *Structure and Vocabulary Aid*, page 76).

One important step in the process of discussion is the *introduction*. The introduction, especially the introductory paragraph, is important for a number of reasons. If it is clearly constructed, it will create a good impression on the reader. A good introduction will not be too long (maximum half a page). It will indicate the structure of the answer or essay by giving an overview of the content in sequence. It may introduce the subject, perhaps with a definition or some historical background etc.

Stage 1   Introductions

1   Below are four introductory paragraphs that might begin the essay title given. All of the paragraphs have been written by native English-speakers.

Read the paragraphs carefully and decide which one you think is the best introduction and why. Discuss with other students to see if you agree.

Introductory Paragraphs

Essay title: 'Discuss the present-day problems facing secondary education in your country.'

a   There are, of course, two sectors of secondary education in England and Wales: the private sector and the state sector. This essay will be concerned only with the latter since it is by far the larger and is faced with many more problems. These
5   can be traced to two important sources: a rapidly changing society and a chronic lack of resources.

b   Secondary education in England is, if not in a mess, in a state of crisis. It faces problems of organisation, partly due to a sharp decrease in the number of pupils and partly due to constant rearguard action by the proponents of selection. It
5   faces problems connected with curriculum development and the reappraisal of the examination system in the attempt to

prepare pupils for the modern world. Finally, it faces problems as a result of government underfunding and, often due to a bad press image, a lack of public confidence.

c   The present structure of state secondary education in England and Wales can be traced back to the Education Act of 1944 which established the school divisions of grammar, technical, and secondary modern. It was as a reaction to the
5   divisive effects of this tripartite system that comprehensive education was introduced in the 1960s. Under the present system all pupils proceed from primary to one kind of secondary school without the need for an examination. In what follows, an attempt will be made to show that most of
10   the present-day problems of secondary education stem from an inadequate provision that was made for the changeover to comprehensive education. 'Inadequate provision' will be shown to relate to the preparation of teachers and the supply and type of school buildings and educational materials.

d   This essay will examine problems facing secondary education in Britain today. It will examine the background to the problems, starting with the 1944 Education Act, which established universal free primary and secondary education. It
5   will then look at problems associated with comprehensive schools. After this, it will examine the concept of the National Curriculum, the extended responsibilities and powers of school governors, the local management of schools, and the principle of schools opting out from local authority control.
10   Finally, there will be an analysis of the relationship between central government and local education authorities, and a discussion of the problems relating to the financing of schools.

2   Now you write an introductory paragraph for the same essay title about your country.

3   There are several different methods of teaching a subject. They can be divided into two broad categories: teacher centred and student centred. Here we shall look at one example of a teacher centred method.

Look at the following notes.

Lecturing as a method of teaching

For	Against
1 Lectures are an economical way of giving information to a large number of students.	1 Lectures are often badly delivered and are boring.
2 The latest information or views can be heard.	2 Often the same lecture notes are used year after year.
3 It is more interesting to hear and see a person than to read a book.	3 It is difficult to take notes in a lecture.
4 A good lecture can stimulate thought and discussion.	4 Many lecturers just read aloud parts of their books. It is easier to read the books.

Can you think of any other arguments to add to the list, *for* or *against*? If so, write them down.

4a   Now read carefully the following passage.

Advantages and disadvantages of the lecturing method

Lecturing as a method of teaching is so frequently under attack today from educational psychologists and by students that some justification is needed to retain it. Critics believe that it results in passive methods of learning which tend to be
5 less effective than those which fully engage the learner. They also maintain that students have no opportunity to ask questions and must all receive the same content at the same pace, that they are exposed only to one teacher's interpretation of subject matter which will inevitably be
10 biased and that, anyway, few lectures rise above dullness. Nevertheless, in a number of inquiries this pessimistic assessment of lecturing as a teaching method proves not to be general among students, although they do fairly often comment on poor lecturing techniques.
15   Students praise lectures which are clear, orderly synopses in which basic principles are emphasised, but dislike too numerous digressions or lectures which consist in part of the contents of a textbook. Students of science subjects consider that a lecture is a good way to introduce a new subject,
20 putting it in its context, or to present material not yet included in books. They also appreciate its value as a period of discussion of problems and possible solutions with their lecturer. They do not look for inspiration—this is more commonly mentioned by teachers—but arts students look for
25 originality in lectures. Medical and dental students who have reported on teaching methods, or specifically on lecturing, suggest that there should be fewer lectures or that, at the least, more would be unpopular.

Here the writer is evaluating the different views held by different groups of students. The style of writing is impersonal. A number of generalisations are used.

b   Now write a paragraph adding your own view of lecturing. You can begin (in the following impersonal way):

> One of the main arguments   against   lecturing is that . . .
> in favour of

Stage 2
'For' and 'Against'

1   Below are some notes on advertising. Making use of the notes, write about advertising, presenting the arguments for and against. Add your own view at the end. You will probably need to compare and contrast and to make qualified generalisations.

Advertising

For	Against
1 Advertisements give up-to-date information about products.	1 Advertisements do not give *information*, they try to persuade us to buy.
2 If there was no advertising consumers would only know about goods in their local shops.	2 They create a demand for goods that are not really needed.
3 Advertising helps to sell to a bigger market. Therefore, as more goods are sold they are cheaper.	3 Advertising adds to the cost of the goods.
4 Advertisements provide revenue for newspapers etc.	4 Advertisements are generally ugly to look at and spoil the environment.

2a Choose one of the following topics to write about. Before you begin, make notes *for* and *against* aspects of the subject. Discuss both sides of the argument, comparing and contrasting. Where necessary make qualified generalisations. You may wish to mention cause and effect. Try to give reasons for your own view at the end.

1 Discuss the function of newspapers.
2 'The biggest problem that the world will face in the 21st century will be related to sources of energy.' Discuss.
3 'Business and pollution are synonymous.' Is this a fair comment? Discuss.
4 Evaluate the main arguments for and against the censorship of films or TV programmes for children.
5 Discuss the proposition that the stability of society is maintained by the family unit.
6 Discuss the problems associated with the recycling of waste material such as newspapers and magazines, glass bottles and drink cans.
7 What are the difficulties in trying to compare the standard of living between countries?

Note: Refer to 'Examination and Essay Questions: Glossary' if necessary (*Appendix 10*, page 125).

b Try to choose some aspects of your own specialised subject to discuss, or a subject in which you are interested.

Structure and Vocabulary Aid

A Points of view may be expressed cautiously or tentatively, or strongly or emphatically (it depends upon your feelings and the purpose of the writing). Agreement or disagreement may be total or partial.

B Below are some ways to express views.

1 *Introducing your own point of view*:

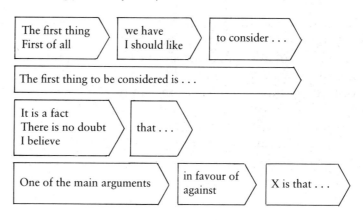

2 *Agreement*:

3 *Partial disagreement*:

    . . . but . . .
    . . . however, . . .
    . . . on the other hand, . . .

4 *Emphatic agreement*:

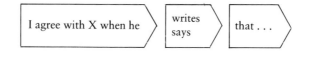

5 *Cautious agreement*:

6 *Disagreement*:

> I disagree with X when he says that . . .

C One way of giving emphasis to what is written is by using a grammatical construction sometimes known as 'negative inversion'. Some of the introductory words are listed below. If they are used, the word order after the introductory words should be *inverted* as in the example:

Rarely had such a noise been heard.   On no account . . .
Never . . .   Seldom . . .
Hardly . . . when . . .   Neither . . .
Not only . . . but also . . .   Few . .
Under no circumstances . . .   Little . . .

Unit 13   Drawing Conclusions

Drawing a *conclusion* often involves making a summary of the main points already made. In addition, one's own opinion or viewpoint may be added, if it is appropriate. A mistake that is sometimes made is to add a conclusion that does not follow logically from what has been written before. (This is sometimes called a 'non-sequitur'.) Avoid doing this! In this unit we practise making concluding remarks.

Before writing any of the exercises look at the *Structure and Vocabulary Aid* at the end of this unit (page 81). Look also at the *Notes on the Exercises* (page 140) for comments on some of the exercises.

Stage 1
Concluding Remarks

1   Turn to Unit 11, Stage 2: *Marriages in England and Wales*.

After commenting on the graph or predicting the number of probable marriages in the future, we might conclude:

'The trend suggests that people are getting less religious (or, more secular), or that marriage is seen more as a social contract and less as a religious ceremony. It may be concluded that although fewer people now get married in a church, there was a reversal of the trend in the 1980s. It is not clear how far that trend will continue.'

2a   Read the following carefully.

Health

It is generally accepted that a dietary intake of about 2500 calories a day is a basic requirement for proper health, of which a particularly important element is the protein content. Therefore, it can be assumed that if the protein intake in the
5   diet falls below a certain level, it will lead to malnutrition and disease. The average adult's body contains about 10.9 kg (24 lb) of protein; only 2.2 kg (5 lb) can be lost without death occurring.

An adult needs to replace about 40 grams (1½ oz) of protein
10   a day. In developed countries nearly everyone gets about twice as much protein as he really needs, often from eating such food as milk, cheese, eggs, fish and meat, all of which are high in protein content. In developing countries, on the other hand, many vegetables that are eaten contain little
15   protein. Some, however, are rich in protein: for example, soya beans.

Table 1: Daily calorie and protein consumption

Country	Daily calorie intake per capita	Daily total protein intake per capita (grams)
U.S.A.	3200	95.6
U.K.	3150	87.5
Mexico	2550	65.7
Japan	2460	74.7
Nigeria	2180	59.3
India	1810	45.4

Source: FAO—'The State of Food and Agriculture'

b Now complete the following.

It can be concluded from the text and *Table 1* that people in the U.S.A. have _____

_____. On the other hand, those in India

_____.

Stage 2
Concluding from Tables

1 Look carefully at the information contained in the tables below.

Table 2: Infant mortality rate per 1000 births

Japan	6	Jordan	54
Finland	6	Saudi Arabia	66
U.K.	10	Indonesia	84
U.S.A.	11	India	105
USSR	25	Nepal	138
Venezuela	26	Nigeria	145
Mexico	53		

Source: UN Demographic Year Book, 1986

Table 3: Medical facilities

Country	Population per hospital bed	Population per physician
Finland	65	480
USSR	80	267
Japan	84	735
U.K.	127	711
U.S.A.	171	549
Venezuela	317	888
India	634	2,545
Saudi Arabia	645	2,606
Jordan	717	1,175
Mexico	863	2,136
Nigeria	1,251	9,591
Indonesia	1,787	11,740
Nepal	5,271	28,767

Source: UN Statistical Year Book, 1984

Table 4: Life expectancy at 5 years

Country	male years	female years
Japan	70	76
U.S.A.	67	74
U.K.	67	73
Finland	65	74
Venezuela	65	70
Mexico	62	66
USSR	60	70
India	58	60
Nepal	55	54
Nigeria	47	50

Source: UN Demographic Year Book, 1986

a From the information contained in *Table 1* together with the information contained in *Tables 2, 3* and *4*, are there any conclusions that you can draw about Japan and Nepal, or any other two countries that you wish to compare?

b With the information that you have from the four tables, are there any general conclusions that you can reach regarding diet, health or life expectancy?

2 Study the following table, which gives information about children killed in road accidents in Britain during May, June and July in one recent year.

Table 5: Road accidents in Britain

When/Where accidents occurred	Age 2–4	Age 5–7	Age 8–11	Age 11–13	Age 14–16	TOTAL
Going to school	2	12	8	2	1	25
Going home from school	2	17	10	3	2	34
Playing in the street	98	81	28	5	2	214
Cycling in the street	1	10	25	8	1	45
Shopping for their parents	5	32	12	2	1	52
TOTAL	108	152	83	20	7	370

Analyse the information in the table above. Comment on the significant items and discuss them. What conclusions can you draw?

Structure and Vocabulary Aid

A Summarising

In short, . . .
In a word, . . .
In brief, . . .
To sum up, . . .

Concluding

In conclusion, . . .
On the whole, . . .
Altogether, . . .
In all, . . .

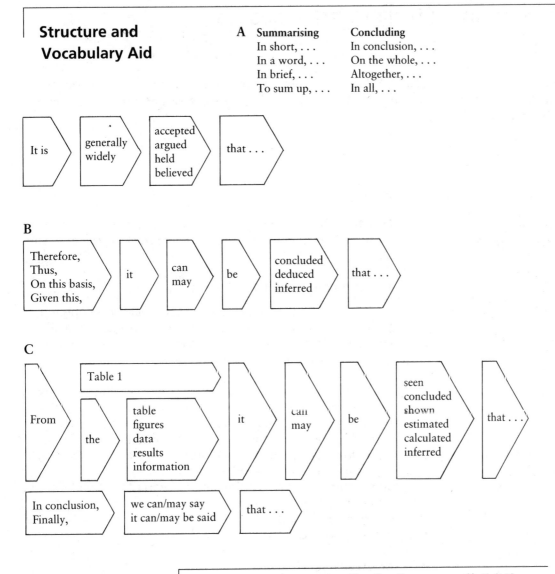

B

C

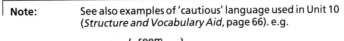

Note: See also examples of 'cautious' language used in Unit 10 (*Structure and Vocabulary Aid*, page 66). e.g.

It would { seem / appear } that . . .

Unit 14   Reports: Studies and Research

Students sometimes need to write reports on their studies or research, often for their sponsors who need to know what progress they are making. Practice is given below in preparing short, straightforward reports.

Stage 1
Reports on Studies

1   Read the following report. Notice, in particular, the verb forms that are used. The report was written in December, at the end of the first term.

A report on my studies this term

I am studying for the Diploma in Economic Development in the Department of Economics. It is a one-year course which consists of lectures, seminars, the writing of essays, and an examination at the end. I started the course at the beginning of October this year. It will finish in June next year.

So far, I have enjoyed the course. However, I have had two kinds of difficulties: one is following some of the lecturers—they speak quickly and not very clearly; the other difficulty is caused by the use of mathematics in economics. I have difficulty in understanding and using some of the equations.

This term I have finished two essays: they were quite long, and required a lot of reading in the library. Although I found it rather difficult to write the essays, I learned a lot, and received good marks for them. Next term I shall have to write another two essays.

2   Now read through the following report. It is similar to the one you have just read, but some changes have been made. Complete the report by writing *one* or *two* words in each space.

A report on my studies

I am (1) _____ for an M.A. in (2) _____ _____ in the Department of (3) _____. It is a one-year course which (4) _____ of lectures, seminars, essays, an examination, and a (5) _____. I (6) _____ the course at the (7) _____ _____ of October last year; the examination will be in June this year, and the dissertation must be (8) _____ in September this year.

Generally, I have enjoyed the course and I feel that I (9) _____ a lot, especially from the reading that I have (10) _____ to do. At (11) _____ I had some difficulties in (12) _____ some of the (13) _____: they spoke quickly and not (14) _____ clearly. The main difficulty that I have this term is (15) _____ my essays on time. There is so

(16) _____ reading to do for them and I still read (17) _____.

I am not looking (18) _____ to the examination as I have difficulty in writing quickly and (19) _____ all the necessary facts. (20) _____ I do not mind doing this dissertation (21) _____ I have already (22) _____ a subject that interests me.

Stage 2
Reports on Research

1 Read through the following report, then complete it by writing one word in each space.

Report on my research

I arrived at the university (1) _____ the beginning of October last year to (2) _____ my studies. I am (3) _____ for a Master's degree in Economics—M.A. (Econ.)—by research. It will take me (4) _____ one and two years to complete.

At the beginning of last term I discussed my research with my (5) _____, Dr. M. Jones, in the Department of Economics. He (6) _____ me to draw up a research outline in the area I had (7) _____ for my research—'A case study in foreign aid to developing countries'. After further (8) _____ with Dr. Jones my outline was approved and accepted by the Faculty of Economics.

My next (9) _____ was to begin reading appropriate books, journals and reports (10) _____ the background section of the research 'A Study of the Literature'. My supervisor's (11) _____ was to keep a set of index cards and write the details of each (12) _____ I read on a card. Thus I have started making a (13) _____ which will be very useful for future reference. It will also (14) _____ me a lot of time when I need to provide one at the (15) _____ of my thesis.

This term I have (16) _____ reading and have also made a draft of the first section of the (17) _____, summarising views on foreign aid to developing countries. I have also started to read (18) _____ on the country I have chosen for my case study—Utopia. I have (19) _____ that many of the World Bank and UN publications are (20) _____ to my research.

I am quite pleased with the (21) _____ I have made so far, although the reading is taking me longer than I (22) _____. My supervisor asked me to present a paper on my research findings up to the present, to a small (23) _____ of research students in economics. He was (24) _____ with the paper and said that it was a good seminar as it had (25) _____ a number of questions and a lot of discussion.

2 Now write a report on your own studies or research. Refer to the *Structure and Vocabulary Aid* (page 86) for help in the structure of the report, and verb tenses that you may need to use.

Stage 3
Report Structures

1 Look at the following structure of a research report. The structure of a dissertation or thesis would be very similar.

Basic framework for a research report

Preliminaries
1 The title
2 Acknowledgements
3 List of contents
4 List of figures/tables

Introduction
5 The abstract
6 Statement of the problem

Main body
7 Review of the literature
8 Design of the investigation
9 Measurement techniques used
10 Results

Conclusion
11 Discussion and conclusion
12 Summary of conclusions

Extras
13 Bibliography
14 Appendices

Note: There may be slight variations to the above. For example, 'The abstract' may be separate and appear at the very beginning of the Report. In its place there may be a section entitled 'Outline of the research'. 9 may be called 'Methods and procedures'. 11 may include 'Recommendations and suggestions for further research'.

2 The fourteen sections of the research report framework are listed again below. Beneath them are explanations of the fourteen sections, lettered **a** to **n** – listed in the wrong order.

Read the explanations carefully and try to decide which explanation is appropriate for each section. Write the letters **a** to **n** next to the numbered sections.

Basic framework for a research report

1 The title
2 Acknowledgements
3 List of contents
4 List of figures/tables
5 The abstract
6 Statement of the problem
7 Review of the literature
8 Design of the investigation
9 Measurement techniques used

10 Results
11 Discussion and conclusion
12 Summary of conclusions
13 Bibliography
14 Appendices

a   the presentation in a logical order of information and data upon which a decision can be made to accept or reject the hypotheses.

b   a compilation of important data and explanatory and illustrative material, placed outside the main body of the text.

c   the sections, in sequence, included in the report.

d   a survey of selective, relevant and appropriate reading, both of primary and secondary source materials. Evidence of original and critical thought applied to books and journals.

e   the presentation of principles, relationships, correlations and generalisations shown by the results. The interpretation of the results and their relationship to the research problem and hypotheses. The making of deductions and inferences, and the implications for the research. The making of recommendations.

f   an accurate listing in strict alphabetical order of all the sources cited in the text.

g   an extremely concise summary of the contents of the report, including the conclusions. It provides an overview of the whole report for the reader.

h   thanking colleagues, supervisors, sponsors, etc. for their assistance.

i   detailed descriptions and discussion of testing devices used. Presentation of data supporting validity and reliability. A discussion of the analysis to be applied to the results to test the hypotheses.

j   a concise account of the main findings, and the inferences drawn from them.

k   a statement and discussion of the hypotheses, and the theoretical structure in which they will be tested and examined, together with the methods used.

l   the sequence of charts or diagrams that appear in the text.

m   the fewest words possible that adequately describe the paper.

n   a brief discussion of the nature of the research and the reasons for undertaking it. A clear declaration of proposals and hypotheses.

Structure and Vocabulary Aid

Report on my studies/research this term.

1 Organise the report so that it is in three paragraphs.
   a *introduction*: outline of studies; the beginning
   b *development*: description/explanation; now
   c *conclusion*: difficulties or success; the future

2 Choose carefully the verb tenses that you will use. Some commonly used verb tenses in reports are:
   present continuous (e.g. I am studying)
   present perfect   (e.g. I have experimented)
   past simple   (e.g. I started)

3 Below are examples of sentences with alternatives that may be useful for your report.

A Introduction

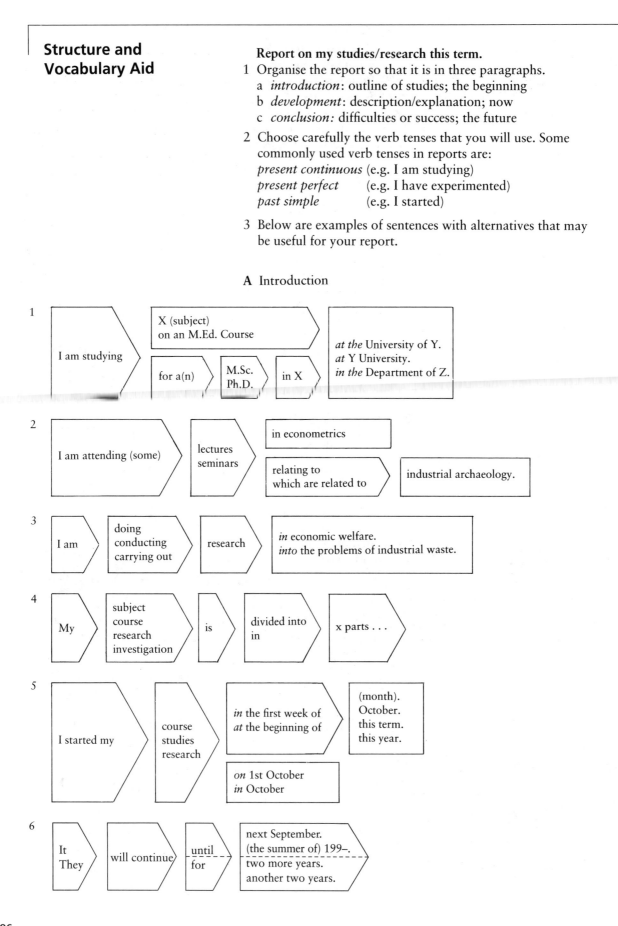

B Development

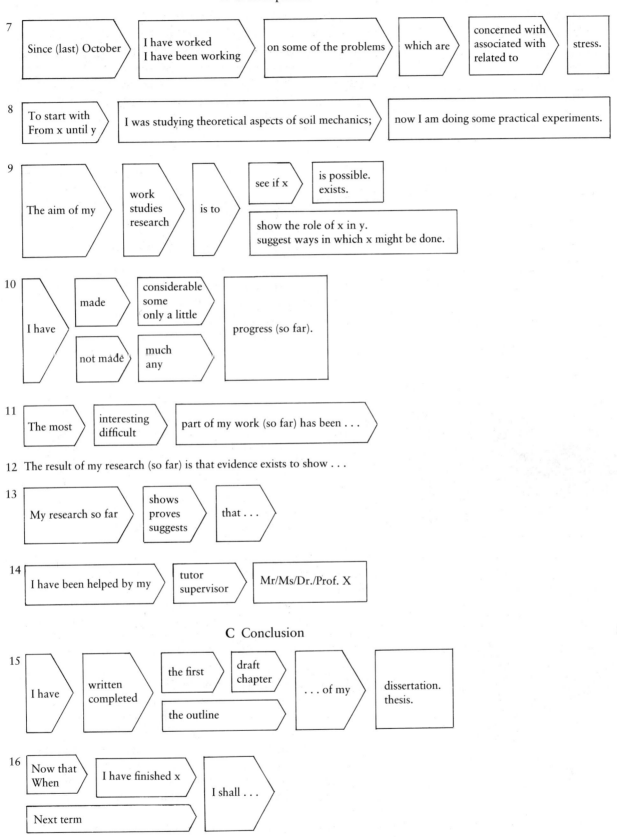

7　Since (last) October ⟩ I have worked / I have been working ⟩ on some of the problems ⟩ which are ⟩ concerned with / associated with / related to ⟩ stress.

8　To start with / From x until y ⟩ I was studying theoretical aspects of soil mechanics; now I am doing some practical experiments.

9　The aim of my ⟩ work / studies / research ⟩ is to ⟩ see if x ⟩ is possible. / exists. / show the role of x in y. / suggest ways in which x might be done.

10　I have ⟩ made / not made ⟩ considerable / some / only a little / much / any ⟩ progress (so far).

11　The most ⟩ interesting / difficult ⟩ part of my work (so far) has been . . .

12　The result of my research (so far) is that evidence exists to show . . .

13　My research so far ⟩ shows / proves / suggests ⟩ that . . .

14　I have been helped by my ⟩ tutor / supervisor ⟩ Mr/Ms/Dr./Prof. X

C Conclusion

15　I have ⟩ written / completed ⟩ the first / draft chapter / the outline ⟩ . . . of my ⟩ dissertation. / thesis.

16　Now that / When ⟩ I have finished x ⟩ / Next term ⟩ I shall . . .

Unit 15 Surveys and Questionnaires

Students in humanities and social sciences at times need to undertake surveys as part of their studies. Questionnaires may be a part of the surveys and the results may be incorporated in a report.

Stage 1 Surveys

1 Read the report below of the survey into the reading habits of students. Notice the verb tenses that are used.

Survey of Academic and General Reading in English

On 8th February 1989, a survey was conducted among 16 overseas postgraduates at the University of Chester. The purpose of the survey was to discover the reading habits in English of the students.

5 The survey was conducted by means of a questionnaire given to the students to complete. The first part of the questionnaire dealt with the type of reading and its frequency. The second section was concerned with newspapers: the type of items read and those that were read
10 first.

From the table of data, the most significant items are as follows. In the first section 81% of the students regularly read academic books, while 44% regularly read academic journals. Nothing else is read regularly or often by 40% or more of the
15 students. The following comments can be made about the reading of newspapers, magazines and fiction. 75% sometimes read regional or local newspapers, 69% sometimes read books of fiction, 62% sometimes read general magazines, and 56% sometimes read national daily
20 newspapers. On the other hand, 37% never read Sunday newspapers and 31% never read fiction.

In the second section, not surprisingly, 100% read news about their own country in newspapers and 56% read this first. 94% read international news, 25% read this first. 81%
25 read about Britain and look at radio and T.V. information. The only other item that is usually read by more than 50% of the students is current affairs (read by 56%).

If any conclusions may be drawn from the data, they are, perhaps, as follows. Overseas students presumably have little
30 time for general reading: most of their reading time is spent on books and journals on their own subject. Outside their studies, apart from reading news about their own country, international news, and news about Britain, they probably spend most time watching T.V. and listening to the radio.

2 If possible, in your class or group, complete the following Survey of Personal Views (it may be necessary to photocopy this page so that

you or your tutor may collect it for purposes of analysis). When the questionnaire has been completed and analysed, write a report of the main findings. You can use the account of the example survey that follows, as a model.

A Survey of Personal Views

On 15th February 1989, an instant survey was carried out among 18 overseas postgraduate students; 11 students were male and 7 were female. The purpose of the survey was to discover the views of the students on a number of matters of
5 personal concern.

The survey was conducted by means of a questionnaire given to the students to complete. There were five questions (with one exception each involved ticking items on a given list). The first question concerned favourite colour, and the
10 second, favourite number. The next three questions were all concerned with aspects of marriage: number three looked at the ideal age to get married, number four examined the qualities looked for in a partner, and number five asked about the ideal number of children.

15 The main findings were as follows. Blue was the most popular colour, chosen by 28%; this was followed by green and purple, each selected by 22% and red with 11%. No-one chose brown, orange or black. There was no real significance in the choice of a lucky number (numbers 3, 6, and 13 each
20 chosen by 11%); 33% of the students said that they had none.

61% of the students selected the age group 26–30 years as ideal for marriage, followed by 21–25 years, chosen by 33%. Only one person did not believe in marriage. In looking at the most important qualities in an ideal partner, 56% wanted the
25 person to be intelligent, 39% chose natural, 33% selected loving, while 28% indicated attractive and honest. No-one chose homely, passionate, generous or serious. The ideal number of children was 2, chosen by 56% followed by 3, selected by 17%, and 1 chosen by 11%. 4 and more than 5
30 children were each selected by 1 student, while no-one indicated no children.

It is not easy to reach any definite conclusions based upon such a small sample of students from such widely differing backgrounds. However, it is clear that a majority favour 26–30
35 as the ideal age to get married with an intelligent partner, and producing 2 children.

A Survey of Personal Views

1 Tick the colour you like best from those listed below.

red	_____	blue	_____
brown	_____	grey	_____
orange	_____	green	_____
yellow	_____	purple	_____
white	_____	black	_____

2 Which is your lucky or favourite number? _____
(if you do not have one, write 'none'.)

3 What do you consider to be the ideal age to get married? Tick one
of the age groups below.

16–20 years	_____	31–35 years	_____	If none of these, state
21–25 „	_____	36–40 „	_____	what you think here.
26–30 „	_____	41–45 „	_____	_____

Note:	If you do not believe in marriage, tick here _____

4 Tick below the *3* most important qualities you would look for in
your ideal partner.

lively	__	thrifty	__	kind	__	generous	__
cheerful	__	homely	__	passionate	__	humorous	__
attractive	__	hard-working	__	loving	__	serious	__
intelligent	__	ambitious	__	romantic	__	reliable	__
honest	__	natural	__	confident	__	faithful	__

5 What do you consider to be the ideal number of children in a
marriage? Tick one of the following.

0	_____	3	_____	
1	_____	4	_____	more than 5 _____
2	_____	5	_____	

Stage 2 Questionnaires

1 Complete the following questionnaire as part of a survey of the
number of hours you and other students in your class or group
spend in studying. When the questionnaire has been completed,
analyse the results and write an account of the main findings as
follows.

Paragraph 1: Introduction

Paragraph 2: Breakdown into sex, age, disciplines

Paragraph 3: Analysis of the total

Paragraph 4: Main differences between disciplines

Paragraph 5: Aspects that you found unusual, unexpected, or
interesting? How you compared with the average?

Paragraph 6: Main conclusions

Survey of Students' Use of Time

Table 1 Studying: subject, level, type

(tick one box in each group)

a   arts/humanities ☐   social sciences ☐

science, technology, ☐   interdisciplinary ☐
medicine

b   undergraduate ☐   postgraduate ☐

other ☐

c   course ☐   research ☐

other ☐

Table 2 Sex and age

a   *circle appropriately*: male / female

b   *tick appropriate age band*:

15–20 ☐		31–35 ☐	
21–25 ☐		36–40 ☐	
26–30 ☐		41+ ☐	

Table 3 Hours spent in studying

	Number of hours per day (average or typical)		TOTAL per day
	timetabled work[1]	informal study[2]	
Monday			
Tuesday			
Wednesday			
Thursday			
Friday			
Saturday			
Sunday			
TOTAL per week			GRAND TOTAL per week

[1] e.g. lectures, seminars, tutorials, supervisions, laboratory classes
[2] e.g. library use, private study, research

2 Optional questionnaire

You and your tutor might like to undertake a questionnaire to provide feedback on this writing course for your tutor's use. Answer the following questions after thinking carefully about your ability at academic writing.

1a Do you think your writing in English has improved at all during this course? YES/NO.

b If the answer is YES, briefly describe what improvements you think you have made.

_____

_____

_____

c If the answer is NO, what do you think are the reasons?

_____

_____

_____

2 Briefly describe any difficulties that you think you still have with academic writing.

_____

_____

3 How relevant and useful, in helping you to improve your writing, have you found this book? (please tick one)

very ☐   reasonably ☐   only just ☐   not very ☐   not at all ☐

4 What kind of writing practice do you think would be most useful for you now?

_____

_____

5 Have you any final comments to make?

_____

_____

_____

Appendices

Appendix 1   Accuracy: Awareness and Correction

The purpose of this Appendix is to examine some of the common types of error that are often made by students when writing formal or academic English. The first step is to be aware that an error has been made; the second step is to recognise or identify it; the third step is to correct it. Of course, it is far better not to make the error in the first place! If you look carefully at what follows it should help you *not* to make some of the mistakes in your writing.

1   Some common causes of error
  a Probably the biggest cause of error is *literal translation* from your own language into English. If you try to translate word for word you will make mistakes.

   For example: in Nepali, the sentence 'John said nothing' would be rendered as (translated) 'John nothing spoke'. It is easy to see that when translating into English the word order and the sentence structure could cause difficulties, and also the vocabulary.

   ADVICE: Try to remember English sentence patterns when you read them and try to use them in your writing.

  b If you write in long complex sentences it is easier to make mistakes: the sentence becomes complicated and the subject and verb tenses may become confused.

   ADVICE: Try to write in fairly short sentences (perhaps at most about three lines) until you are confident that there are no mistakes.

  c If you try to write English in the same way as you speak it, you will probably write in the wrong *style*. Spoken language is often *informal*. Academic writing is normally rather *formal* (see pages 101–102).

   ADVICE: Try to recognise a formal style of writing and use it. Do not mix it with an informal style.

2 Some common types of error

a Subject and verb agreement (i.e. concord); particularly singular and plural subject with the correct verb form. E.g. they were (*not* 'they was') (see Appendix 6 page 114).

b The use of *s* at the end of the third person singular, present simple tense (i.e. stem + s). E.g. the writer says (*not* 'the writer say').

c 1 *This* + singular noun, *these* + plural noun;
   2 *Other* and *another* differences.
   (See **Grammar** exercises on page 98 and explanation.)

d Uncountable nouns are often wrongly used (as if they were countable nouns). E.g. This information is useful (*not* 'These informations are useful').

e When the impersonal *It* or *There* subject should be used, it is often wrongly omitted. E.g. It seems that we should . . . (*not* 'Seems that we . . .').

f Verb tense use confused, particularly the present continuous (used too frequently) and present simple. E.g. I work in the library every day (*not* 'I am working in . . .').

g The formation of some verb tenses is not known, particularly the present passive. The formation of the past tenses of irregular verbs also causes difficulty. (See Appendix 4, page 110).

h *No* and *not* differences in using the negatives. (See **Grammar** exercises on page 98 and explanation).

i The formation and use of some of the comparative and superlative forms of adjectives and adverbs. (See Unit 8, page 49 and Appendix 7, page 116).

j The correct use of: 1 some prepositions: (e.g. *in, on, at, for*)
                        2 the articles: *a/an/the*
                        3 relative pronouns: *who, which*
                        4 possessive adjectives: *his, her, their*.

k Confusion over the choice of vocabulary, e.g. *make* and *do*. The choice of synonyms will often depend on *usage* (or *context*) as much as on meaning. (See **Vocabulary** on page 99).

l Spelling mistakes. (See the next section, **Spelling**, page 95).

3 Practice in areas of language difficulty

The following sections will give you practice in some of the areas of language that commonly cause difficulty; these were noted above. The main areas are:

> Spelling and Punctuation
> Grammar and Vocabulary
> Style and Appropriateness

The practice given here can only be brief. If you find that you still make a number of errors or have difficulty after completing the exercises, look at the references given in the *Guide to Using the Book* (page 7). The books referred to there give more practice in areas of difficulty.

a Each time you do an exercise and practise the language you should be as *accurate* as possible: copy carefully.

b If you make a mistake, learn from it. Try not to repeat an error.

c Do not forget the seemingly simple or obvious elements in writing, e.g. write as legibly or clearly as possible. Remember, if someone cannot *read* your writing it does not matter how accurate it is!

d Check your *punctuation*: if you have used a full-stop /./ it indicates the end of a sentence and immediately after it the next sentence will begin with a capital letter.

e Do *not* mix capital letters and small letters within a word: it gives the impression that you are uneducated!

f Remember to divide your writing into *paragraphs*: it makes it easier to read and creates a better impression.

Spelling

Exercise 1   Recognition

Each word in CAPITAL LETTERS to the left of the line is spelled correctly. The same word is repeated correctly *once* in small letters in the list of four words to the right of the line. Draw a circle around each word to the right of the line that is the *same* as the word to the left: e.g.

5 BELIEVE   beleve   belief   (believe)   beleve

or write the correct letter next to each number: e.g. **C**5.

1 If you have difficulty with English spelling or writing, do the exercise by looking carefully at the word in capital letters and try to match it with one of the words in small letters.

2 If you think you do not have much difficulty with English spelling or writing, look first at the word in capital letters and then cover it up before you look at the words in small letters.

	A	**B**	**C**	**D**
1 ACCOMMODATION	acommodation	accomodation	accommodation	acomodation
2 ACHIEVE	acheve	achieve	acheive	achive
3 APPLICABLE	applicible	aplicable	applicable	applicabel
4 BEGINNING	biginning	beginning	begining	beggining
5 CHOICE	choise	chose	choose	choice
6 CRITICISM	criticicm	criticism	critisism	critism
7 DEVELOPMENT	developement	divelopment	development	divelopement
8 DISAPPEARED	disapeared	dissappeared	dissapeared	disappeared
9 DIVIDED	diveded	divedid	devided	divided
10 EMPHASIS	emphasis	emphases	emphasise	emphisis
11 EXPERIMENTAL	expiremental	experemental	experimental	expirimental
12 FOREIGNER	foreigner	foriegner	forienger	foreinger
13 FREQUENTLY	friquently	frequantly	frecuently	frequently
14 GOVERNMENT	goverment	government	governement	goverement
15 HEIGHT	heigt	height	heigth	hieght
16 HYPOTHESIS	hypophysis	hypotheses	hypothesis	hypophesis
17 INCREASINGLY	increasingly	incresingly	increaseingly	increasingely
18 INSUFFICIENT	insuffcent	insuficient	insufficient	insuffecient
19 INTERESTING	intresting	intiresting	interisting	interesting
20 INTERVIEWED	interviwed	interwiewed	interveiwed	interviewed
21 KNOWLEDGE	knowlege	knowledge	knoledge	nowledge
22 LABOURERS	labours	laborers	labourers	laboures
23 MAINTAINING	maintaning	mantaining	maintianing	maintaining
24 MEDICINE	medisine	medecine	medesine	medicine

	A	B	C	D
25 NECESSARY	necessary	necesary	neccesary	neccessary
26 OCCUPATION	occuppation	occupation	ocupation	ocuppation
27 OCCURRED	occured	ocurred	ocured	occurred
28 PREDOMINANTLY	predominantly	predominately	predominatly	predominently
29 RAISED	riased	rised	raised	araised
30 REFERRING	referring	refering	reffering	refereeing
31 RESEARCH	reserch	research	reaserch	risearch
32 RESOURCES	resourses	resources	risources	resorses
33 SCHOOLS	shools	scools	school	schools
34 STUDYING	stuyding	studing	studying	istudying
35 SUCCESSFUL	succesful	successful	sucessful	successfull
36 TECHNIQUES	techniques	technics	technicues	teckniques
37 THOROUGH	thorought	thorough	through	trough
38 WHETHER	wether	weather	wheather	whether
39 WHICH	whitch	wich	witch	which
40 WRITING	writeing	writting	writing	wraiting

Now check your answers with those given on page 142.

Exercise 2   Correction

The following 10 words are all spelled *wrongly*. You have already seen them spelled *correctly* in Exercise 1. Without looking back at Exercise 1 write out the 10 words correctly.

1	acheve	6	maintaning
2	freqantly	7	medecine
3	incresingely	8	reaserch
4	insuffcent	9	reffering
5	interveiwed	10	sucessfull

Now check your answers on page 142.

Exercise 3   Correction

The following 10 words are all spelled *wrongly*. Many of the mistakes are similar to the mistakes shown in Exercise 1. Try to write the words correctly. If you have great difficulty use a dictionary, but only after you have attempted the correction by yourself.

1	seperatly	6	conscioseness
2	prefered	7	embarassed
3	recieve	8	preceed
4	recomendasion	9	discucion
5	enviroment	10	caracteristics

Now check your answers on page 142.

Note: For extra information on sounds and spelling see *Appendix 2: Sounds and Spelling* (page 104).

Punctuation

The most commonly used punctuation marks and their names are as follows:

comma /,/ full-stop /./ colon /:/ semi-colon /;/ hyphen

apostrophe (John's) question mark /?/ dash /—/

quotation marks (or inverted commas) /" "/ or /' '/
exclamation mark /!/ brackets (or parentheses) ( )

Note: See *Appendix 3* (page 107) for guidance on the use of punctuation marks and capital letters.

Exercise 1
In the following passage put the correct punctuation marks in the spaces underlined. Also add capital letters where necessary.

the first of the great civic universities established in england _ manchester is today the largest unitary university in the united kingdom and an internationally famous centre of learning and research _ it is well _ endowed with resources and facilities   the university library   for instance _ is one of the four big academic libraries in the country _ and the university has its own modern theatre _ television studios _ art gallery _ museum _ shopping centre and _ of course _ extensive sports facilities _

Now turn to page 142 and check your answers.

Exercise 2
Now copy out the passage below putting in the correct punctuation marks. Remember to use capital letters where appropriate.

mr brown had been teaching english abroad for a number of years he had forgotten how cold it could be in england in the winter it was often dull and grey in november but it could be really cold in december january and february even in the spring it could snow mr brown looked out of the window as the train crossed the river avon he remembered the weather forecast that he had heard on the bbc at 9 oclock that tuesday morning it had said that it would be wet and windy in the north west manchester where he was now travelling to was unfortunately in the north west

Now turn to page 143 for the answers.

Grammar

Some areas of language consistently cause difficulty. Some of the main ones have been selected below for practice.

1 In the sentences below there are a number of errors: they have been underlined. On the lines beneath each sentence write the whole sentence *correctly*. The first one is started for you.

a Table 3 is showing that most of this accidents occurs to young children.
  Table 3 shows that most of these accidents occur to young children.

b Each worker pay a small money which is taken from their salary.

c Specialist doctors in hospitals can divide into surgeons which operate _____ the body and another specialists which act as consultants.

d The number of schools growed gradually till 1965 and then _____ number rised suddenly.

e When a country apply for foreign aids, _____ is because it has no enough resources of its own.

Turn to page 143 for the answers and for an explanation of the errors.

2 In the sentences below there are a number of errors: many of them are similar to the errors made in Section 1. First underline the error and then write the whole sentence *correctly* on the lines provided.

a If somebody become ill, then can go to local doctor.

b To my opinion, there is many parent which did not take care their children.

c In the other hand, if we look the table of accidents, we will see this facts.

d In my country we have other kind of system; it is bigger and more better.

Turn to page 143 for the answers and for an explanation of the errors.

e The problem was solve by the introduction of machineries.

Vocabulary

Vocabulary is a very large subject. It really requires a book to itself; in other words a dictionary. In fact, a good mono-lingual English dictionary is the best book that you, as a student of English, can buy. Recommended ones, especially compiled for the student of English are:

Collins COBUILD English Language Dictionary—Collins
Longman Dictionary of Contemporary English—Longman.
Oxford Advanced Learner's Dictionary—O.U.P.

Often a wrong word is used because a wrong choice has been made between similar words or *synonyms*. The choice of synonyms will often depend on usage, or context, as much as on meaning. A good English dictionary will give examples of usage or context that will help you to choose the correct word.

Some attention is given below to a few words that frequently cause difficulty to students. Read the information and examples carefully.

1 Verbs

a Make and Do

The basic meanings are: *make*: construct, produce, form, shape, create.
do: perform, carry out, act.

However, there are large lists of idiomatic expressions containing these two verbs; they can be found in the dictionaries referred to above.

Look at these examples.

Considerable progress has been *made* with the experiment.
He found that he could not *do* the research.
He *made* a number of attempts to finish the work.
She had some difficulty in *doing* her homework.
Many discoveries have been *made* this century.

b Rise, Arise, Raise, Increase

rise: (intransitive, i.e. without a direct object) go up, get up, go higher.
e.g. Prices continue to *rise*.
The cost of living index *rose* by 10% last year.
The sun usually *rises* at 5 a.m. in the summer.

Note: *Rise* is also a noun, meaning an increase.
e.g. There was a *rise* in prices caused by a *rise* in wages.

arise: (intransitive) come into existence, appear.
e.g. A new problem has *arisen* in the college.
An unexpected difficulty *arose* when he was analysing the results.

raise: (transitive, i.e. takes a direct object) lift up, make higher, cause to rise.
e.g. Bus fares were *raised* three times last year.
The landlord said he is going to *raise* the rent.
Also: 1 to bring up for discussion or attention.
e.g. He *raised* a new point in the seminar.

2 to manage to get; obtain.

e.g. He *raised* a loan. He tried to *raise* money for a new project.

increase: (transitive and intransitive) make or become greater in size, number, degree, etc.

e.g. The Chancellor of the Exchequer *increased* the tax on petrol in his last Budget.

The population has *increased* by 200 000 to a total of 50 million.

Note: a *increase* can sometimes be used instead of *raise* or *rise*.

e.g. in the above two sentences *raised* could be used in the first and *has risen* in the second.

b *increase* is also a noun, meaning rise.

e.g. There was a steady *increase* in population.

2 **Pairs of words often confused**

NOUN	VERB	NOUN	ADJECTIVE
practice	practise	politics	political
advice	advise	mathematics	mathematical
effect	affect	statistics	statistical
choice	choose	*logic*	logical
		economics	*economic*

ADJECTIVE	VERB
loose	lose

Note: a the adjective *economical* relates to *saving money*, not to the *economy*.

b two adjectives are often confused, partly because of spelling mistakes: *later* (late, later, latest) and *latter* (the second of two things already mentioned; contrasted with *former*, meaning the first of two).

c two adverbs are often confused: *very* (to give emphasis, e.g. very good) and *too* (excessively, e.g. too expensive).

3 **Exercise**

In the spaces in the following sentences write the correct form of the appropriate word in brackets.

a He _____ a big effort to finish in time. (do/make)

b The painting was _____ by a famous artist. (do/make)

c His supervisor _____ him to prepare a talk. (tell/say)

d It is possible to _____ four books at a time from the library. (lend/borrow)

e The oil crisis _____ the price of petrol. (rise/arise/raise)

f Last year the price of food _____ by 15%. (rise/arise/raise)

g Tutors often give good _____ (advice/advise) but students sometimes _____ (choice/choose) not to follow it.

h Of _____ (mathematics/mathematical) and _____ (politics/political), the former is, perhaps, more _____ (logic/logical) than the _____. (later/latter)

Now check your answers with those given on pages 144.
If you have made any mistakes look again carefully at sections 1 and 2 above; if necessary, look at *Irregular Verbs (Appendix 5)*, page 112.

Style and Appropriateness

Written English, in the same way as spoken English, may be formal or informal. The style of writing that we are concerned with in this book is *formal* and mainly academic (other formal styles are official and business).

The differences between spoken and written English can best be seen from a number of examples. In general, informal spoken English contains a number of colloquialisms (conversational expressions) that are inappropriate for formal written English. It is important *not* to mix styles.

1 Written academic English will *not* normally contain the following:
a **Contractions** (i.e. 'it did not' would be used instead of *it didn't*; 'they have' would be used and not *they've*.)
b **Hesitation Fillers** (i.e. *er, um, well, you know* . . . which might be common in the spoken language are omitted.)
c **Familiar Language** that would not be appropriate in the academic context. For example:
   1 A number of phrasal or prepositional verbs are more suitable or appropriate in an informal style, i.e.

FORMAL	INFORMAL
conduct	carry out
discover	find out
investigate	look into

2 Personal pronouns *I, you, we* tend not to be used in more formal writing (except in letters etc.). Instead the style may be more *impersonal*. An introductory *it* or *there* may begin sentences or even the impersonal pronoun *one*; passive tenses may also be used.

2a Compare the following examples of letters: the first very informal, the second formal. Both are replies to invitations. Clearly, the relationship between the writer of a letter and the recipient will determine the style.

Informal
Dear Fred,
   Thanks a lot for the invitation. I'm afraid Sue is ill so we won't be able to come. See you soon.
          All the best,
             Tom

Formal

Dear Professor Smith,

   Thank you very much for the kind invitation to dinner. I regret that my wife is ill so that it will not be possible for us to come. I do hope, however, that I shall have an opportunity of seeing you again in the near future.

Yours sincerely,
Tom Jackson

b Compare the following explanations or definitions of *economics*: the first informal and spoken, the second formal and written (from an economics textbook).

Informal/Spoken

Economics? . . . Yes, well, um . . . economics is, I suppose, about people trying to . . . let me see . . . match things that are scarce—you know—with things that they want, . . . oh yes, and how these efforts have an effect on each other . . . through exchange, I suppose.

Formal/Written

Economics is the social science that studies how people attempt to accommodate scarcity to their wants and how these attempts interact through exchange.

3 **Exercise**

The following sentences are mixed *formal* and *informal*. Write F (formal) or I (informal) in the brackets after each sentence.

a The project will be completed next year. ( )
b I showed that his arguments did not hold water. ( )
c I wonder why he put up with those terrible conditions
   for so long. ( )
d Five more tests will be necessary before the experiment
   can be concluded. ( )
e It is possible to consider the results from a different viewpoint. ( )
f It has been proved that the arguments so far are without
   foundation. ( )
g He'll have to do another five tests before he can stop the
   experiment. ( )
h It is not clear why such terrible conditions were tolerated
   for so long. ( )
i There are a number of reasons why the questionnaire
   should be revised. ( )
j We'll finish the job next year. ( )

Now turn to page 144 and check your answers.

4 A feature of written academic English is the need to be careful (i.e. to indicate 'less than one hundred per cent certainty'). The purpose of such writing is to show that one is generalising or desires to be cautious, or even that one *might possibly* be wrong (though it is not *likely*!).

Note: The three preceding words in italics are examples of such language in use.

The most usual ways of expressing caution or lack of certainty are by means of verbs (e.g. appears to/seems to/tends to/may/might) and adverbs (e.g. perhaps/possibly/probably/apparently). For an explanation of this see Unit 10 (page 62).

a   The following sentence is a *definite* statement:
   Industrialisation is viewed as a superior way of life.

b   To make it more *tentative* or *cautious* we can change or add some words:
   Industrialisation *tends to* be viewed as a superior way of life.

5   **Exercise**

Now look at the following sentences taken from an economics book:

a   It *is* also *likely to* appear in the development of institutions . . .

b   The ideal of economic development *tends to* be associated with different policy goals . . .

c   *Perhaps* greater clarity can be brought to the meaning of economic development . . .

How would the above three sentences be written if we wanted to make them *definite* and *not* tentative?

When you have written the three sentences, turn to page 144 and check your answers.

Appendix 2   Sounds and Spelling

Below the *sounds* of English (represented by phonetic symbols) are shown together with different ways of *spelling* those sounds.

This list may help to find a word in the dictionary that you have heard but not seen.

---

1 Consonants

SOUND	SPELLING
p	<u>p</u>i<u>p</u>, sha<u>p</u>e, wra<u>pp</u>ing
b	mo<u>b</u>, ru<u>bb</u>ing, ro<u>b</u>e

Note: the letter 'b' is silent:
a when *final* after the sound /m/ as in: lamb, limb, climb, bomb, comb, tomb, womb, crumb, dumb, numb, plumb(er), succumb, thumb
b *before* the sound /t/ as in: debt, doubt, subtle

SOUND	SPELLING
t	<u>t</u>each, wri<u>tt</u>en, wri<u>t</u>e, fri<u>ght</u>, passed

Note: parted = /pɑːtɪd/

SOUND	SPELLING
d	<u>d</u>i<u>d</u>, la<u>dd</u>er, ro<u>d</u>e, stay<u>ed</u>

Note: added = /ædɪd/

SOUND	SPELLING
k	<u>c</u>ome, <u>k</u>ing, ba<u>ck</u>, ta<u>k</u>e, tre<u>kk</u>ing, <u>ch</u>aracter, <u>c</u>on<u>qu</u>er, a<u>ch</u>e, bis<u>c</u>uit, toba<u>cc</u>o

Note: a before letters 'e,i,y,' the letter 'c' is pronounced /s/
b the letters 'qu' are usually pronounced /kw/ as in: queen, quick, etc. (**but note**: queue /kjʌ/)
c the letter 'k' is silent in the initial combination 'kn' e.g. knee, knife, knit, knock, knot, know, knuckle

SOUND	SPELLING
g	<u>g</u>o, e<u>gg</u>, <u>g</u>uard

Note: a the letter 'g' is silent, usually in the combination 'gn' in initial or final position e.g. gnash, gnat, gnaw; campaign, reign, sign
b the letter 'g' is silent in the combination 'ough'. The letters 'ough' are pronounced differently in each of the following words: although, bough, cough, enough, thorough, thought, through

SOUND	SPELLING
m	<u>m</u>ay, la<u>m</u>e, thu<u>mb</u>, swi<u>mm</u>ing, colu<u>mn</u>
n	<u>n</u>ow, li<u>n</u>e, begi<u>nn</u>ing, <u>kn</u>ight, <u>gn</u>ome
ŋ	si<u>ng</u>, to<u>ng</u>ue, ha<u>n</u>dkerchief, si<u>n</u>k, a<u>n</u>ger

Note: before the sounds /k/ and /g/ the letter 'n' is pronounced /ŋ/

SOUND	SPELLING
l	<u>l</u>ive, fe<u>ll</u>, mi<u>l</u>e

Note: the letter 'l' is silent in a number of words; some of the commonest are: calf, half, halves, chalk, stalk, talk, walk, folk, yolk, palm, psalm, could, should, would, almond, salmon

SOUND	SPELLING
f	fine, off, safe, philosophy, laugh; there are a number of other words ending in 'gh' e.g. cough, enough, rough, tough
v	vote, save, of
θ	thin
ð	this, breathe
s	sits, writes, house, hissing, cellar, civil, cycle, scene, fasten, psychology (the letter 'p' is silent)

Note: the letter 'c' is only pronounced /s/ before letters 'e,i,y'

| z | zoo, fizzy, laze, deserve, praise, scissors |

Note: Mrs. = /mɪsɪz/ , houses = /haʊzɪz/

ʃ	shoe, sugar, issue, mansion, mission, nation, suspicion, ocean, conscious, machine, fuchsia, schedule (also pronounced /skedu:l/), moustache
ʒ	leisure, confusion, seizure, usual
r	red, berry, rhyme, wrist

Note: the letter 'r' is only pronounced /r/ when the sound following it is a *vowel sound*

| h | hat, who |

Note: the letter 'h' is silent:
   a before a strongly stressed vowel, as in: hour, heir, honour, honest
   b in the combinations 'kh' and 'rh' and 'gh' e.g. khaki, rhyme, ghost
   c in some other words e.g. shepherd

tʃ	church, matches, nature, question
dʒ	jump, gender, age, bridge, judgment, soldier, procedure, adjust
w	well, quick, one, once, choir

Note: a the letter 'w' is silent in the group 'wr' as in: write, wreck, wring, wrist, wrong
   b the letter 'w' is also silent in words such as: two, answer, sword, and in: who, whom, whose, whole
   c when the letter 'w' occurs in the final position it is not pronounced but forms part of the final vowel or diphthong sound e.g. low, cow

| j | yes, opinion, hideous |

Note: when the letters 'i' or 'e' occur before the sound /ə/ then the sound /j/ is used, as in the words: opinion, hideous

2 Vowels

iː		green, these, mean, field, receive, police, key, quay, people
ɪ		cities, busy, become, women, private, England, build, carriage, valley, coffee
e		send, head, friend, said, says, any, bury, leisure
æ		back (plait)
ɑː		far, half, example, are, aunt, heart, clerk
ɒ		hot, want, because, cough, knowledge
ɔː		saw, sauce, nor, more, board, four, tall, war, walk, door, broad, ought
ʊ		push, book, could, woman
uː		rule, blue, feud, new, fruit, food, group, two, too, lose, beauty, shoe, through
ʌ		nut, son, touch, does, blood
ɜː		her, fir, fur, fern, earth, work, journey, were
ə	a	in weakly stressed syllables in an initial or medial position: about, breakfast, particularly, pavement, modern, horrible, method, effort, cupboard, column, famous
	b	in weakly stressed syllables in the final position before a pause: china, collar, letter, doctor, colour, borough, nature, centre

3 Diphthongs

eɪ	game, rain, day, they, vein, great, eight, gaol, gauge, straight
əʊ	go, toe, loaf, grow, shoulder, oh, brooch, mauve, sew
aɪ	bite, sight, try, tie, height, either, buy, eye, aisle, dye, guide
aʊ	found, brown, plough
ɔɪ	voice, boy
ɪə	deer, dear, here, pier, idea, weird
eə	fair, wear, care, where, their, scarce, heir, aeroplane, prayer
ʊə	tour, cure, doer, during, newer, cruel

Appendix 3 Punctuation and Capital Letters

| 1 Main uses of punctuation marks | The following passage shows the main punctuation marks in use. |

question mark

inverted commas/quotation marks —
semi-colon —
capital letters —

exclamation mark —
apostrophe —

"Why study English?" is the title
of a book; it is also a question.
An English-speaking pupil, or a
student, might answer "Because
I've got to!"—especially if
they are at school (where it
is part of the syllabus;
compulsory until the age of
sixteen).

full stop
hyphen
comma
dash
brackets
colon

a **comma /,/**
Together with the full-stop the comma is the most commonly used punctuation mark. Basically it separates parts of the sentence. It is used:
1 to separate a non-defining relative clause from the rest of the sentence.
   e.g. It is years since I read *Anna Karenina*, which is my favourite novel.
2 when a subordinate clause comes before the principal clause.
   e.g. If you do not understand, please tell me.
3 to separate phrases in apposition from the rest of the sentence.
   e.g. Mr Gorbachev, the President, said . . .
4 to separate some non-defining adjectival phrases from the rest of the sentence.
   e.g. The speaker, getting to his feet, began to . . .
5 in many kinds of lists.
   e.g. I shall need a book, some paper, a pencil, and a ruler.
6 to separate a number of connectives from the rest of the sentence: too, however, nevertheless, though, of course, then, etc.
   e.g. You can, however, do it if you wish.
7 when some adverbs or adverbial expressions are placed within a sentence (instead of at the beginning or end of the sentence).
   e.g. They tried, in spite of my advice, to climb the mountain.

b **full-stop /./**
A full stop is used to end a sentence. The next sentence begins with a capital letter.

c colon / : /

A colon is a rather infrequent punctuation mark. It indicates a fairly close interdependence between the units that it separates.

1 Basically, it indicates that what follows it is an explanation or amplification of what precedes it.

e.g. I have some news for you: John's father has arrived.

2 It can be used to introduce a list of items, often preceded by *namely*, *such as*, *as follows*, etc.

e.g. Please send the items indicated below, namely:

(i) passport (ii) visa application (iii) correct fee.

d semi-colon / ; /

1 A semi-colon coordinates or joins two independent but related clauses or sentences.

e.g. The lecture was badly delivered; it went on far too long as well.

2 It is used in lists to show sub-groupings.

e.g. The chief commodities are: butter, cheese, milk, eggs; lamb, beef, veal, pork; oats, barley, rye and wheat.

Note: Normally a full-stop can be used instead of a semi-colon.

e hyphen / - /

1 A hyphen separates, in some cases, the prefix from the second part of the word.

e.g. co-opt

2 It joins some compound words

e.g. self-control, twenty-one

Note: You should always check in a dictionary to see if a hyphen is needed.

f apostrophe / ' /

An apostrophe is most frequently used to indicate genitive (possessive) singular and plural.

e.g. the student's, the students'

Child's, Children's

It is also used in contractions to indicate letters omitted.

e.g. I've = I have

didn't = did not

g question mark / ? /

A question mark is used after a direct question.

e.g. What time is it?

It is *not* used after an indirect question.

e.g. Please tell me what time it is.

h dash / − /

A dash is used to indicate a break, often informally.

e.g. He received a prize − and a certificate as well.

Note: Generally, it is better to avoid using a dash in academic writing.

i quotation marks (quotes) or **inverted commas**: they may be single / ' ' / or double / " " /

They enclose the actual words of direct speech.

e.g. He said, "Why did you do that?"

j exclamation mark / ! /
An exclamation mark is not often used. It is usually only used after real exclamations and sometimes after short commands.
e.g. Oh dear! Get out!

k brackets (parentheses): /( )/
1 Brackets are used to clarify, or to avoid confusion.
  e.g. He (Mr Brown) told him (Mr Jones) that he (Mr Green) had been accepted for the job.
2 They are also used for cross-references and some periods of time, in more formal writing.
  e.g. William Smith (1910–1969) lived first in Manchester (see p. 70) and then . . .

2 Capital Letters

These are used:
a At the beginning of a sentence.
b For names of people, places, rivers, etc.
  e.g. John, Vienna, the Rhine.
c For titles of people and names of things and places when referring to particular examples.
  e.g. a city, *but* the City of Manchester   Mr Jones
      Miss Smith   Mrs Brown   Ms White   Dr Green
      Professor Williams
d For nations and adjectives of nationality.
  e.g. the Netherlands, a Dutchman, Dutch
e For names of days, months, festivals, and historical eras.
  e.g. Monday, January, Christmas, Ramadan, the Middle Ages
f For titles of books, plays, works of art, etc.
  e.g. Animal Farm, Hamlet, the Mona Lisa
g For many abbreviations.
  e.g. R.S.V.P., Ph.D.

Appendix 4 The Tenses Of A Regular Verb: 'To Help'

Active Voice

Infinitive: help   *Past Tense*: helped
Present Participle: helping   *Past Participle*: helped
Imperative: help

Note: Only persons *I*, *he*, *they* are given; *you*, *we* are the same as *they*; *she*, *it* are the same as *he*.

1 Present:

Simple	*Continuous*	*Perfect*
I help	I am helping	I have helped
he helps	he is helping	he has helped
they help	they are helping	they have helped

2 Past:

Simple	*Continuous*	*Perfect*
I helped	I was helping	I had helped
he helped	he was helping	he had helped
they helped	they were helping	they had helped

3 Future:

Simple	*Continuous*	*Perfect*
I shall help	I shall be helping	I shall have helped
he will help	he will be helping	he will have helped
they will help	they will be helping	they will have helped

4 Conditional (Future in the Past):

Simple	*Continuous*	*Perfect*
I would help	I would be helping	I would have helped
he would help	he would be helping	he would have helped
they would help	they would be helping	they would have helped

Passive Voice

Infinitive: be helped   *Present Participle*: being helped
Past Participle: having been helped

1 Present:

Simple	*Continuous*	*Perfect*
I am helped	I am being helped	I have been helped
he is helped	he is being helped	he has been helped
they are helped	they are being helped	they have been helped

2 Past:

Simple	*Continuous*	*Perfect*
I was helped	I was being helped	I had been helped
he was helped	he was being helped	he had been helped
they were helped	they were being helped	they had been helped

3 **Future:**

Simple
I shall be helped
he will be helped
they will be helped

Perfect
I shall have been helped
he will have been helped
they will have been helped

4 **Conditional** (Future in the Past):

Simple
I would be helped
he would be helped
they would be helped

Perfect
I would have been helped
he would have been helped
they would have been helped

Note: The Passive 3 Future: Continuous (e.g. I shall be being helped) and 4 Conditional: Continuous (e.g. I should be being helped), are not often used. The Subjunctive tenses: Past Simple (If I were helped) and Perfect (If I had been helped) are used less frequently than the tenses listed above.

Appendix 5 Irregular Verbs

Infinitive	Past Tense	Past Participle
arise	arose	arisen
awake	awoke	awaked, awoken
be	was	been
bear	bore	borne
beat	beat	beaten
become	became	become
begin	began	begun
behold	beheld	beheld
bend	bent	bent
bet	bet, betted	bet, betted
bid	bade, bid	bidden, bid
bind	bound	bound
bite	bit	bitten
bleed	bled	bled
blow	blew	blown
break	broke	broken
breed	bred	bred
bring	brought	brought
build	built	built
burn	burnt, burned	burnt, burned
burst	burst	burst
buy	bought	bought
catch	caught	caught
choose	chose	chosen
come	came	come
cost	cost	cost
creep	crept	crept
cut	cut	cut
deal	dealt	dealt
dig	dug	dug
dive	dived	dived
do	did	done
draw	drew	drawn
dream	dreamed, dreamt	dreamed, dreamt
drink	drank	drunk
drive	drove	driven
eat	ate	eaten
fall	fell	fallen
feed	fed	fed
feel	felt	felt
fight	fought	fought
find	found	found
flee	fled	fled
fling	flung	flung
fly	flew	flown
forbid	forbade, forbad	forbidden
forecast	forecast, forecasted	forecast, forecasted
foresee	foresaw	foreseen
forget	forgot	forgotten
forgive	forgave	forgiven
freeze	froze	frozen
get	got	got

Infinitive	Past Tense	Past Participle
give	gave	given
go	went	gone
grind	ground	ground
grow	grew	grown
hang	hung	hung
hang	hanged	hanged
have	had	had
hear	heard	heard
hide	hid	hidden, hid
hit	hit	hit
hold	held	held
hurt	hurt	hurt
keep	kept	kept
kneel	knelt	knelt
know	knew	known
lay	laid	laid
lead	led	led
lean	leant, leaned	leant, leaned
leap	leapt, leaped	leapt, leaped
learn	learnt, learned	learnt, learned
leave	left	left
lend	lent	lent
let	let	let
lie	lay	lain
light	lit, lighted	lit, lighted
lose	lost	lost
make	made	made
mean	meant	meant
meet	met	met
mistake	mistook	mistaken
pay	paid	paid
put	put	put
read	read	read
ride	rode	ridden
ring	rang	rung
rise	rose	risen
run	ran	run
saw	sawed	sawn
say	said	said
see	saw	seen
seek	sought	sought
sell	sold	sold
send	sent	sent
set	set	set
shake	shook	shaken
shine	shone	shone
shoot	shot	shot
show	showed	shown, showed
shut	shut	shut
sing	sang	sung
sink	sank	sunk
sit	sat	sat
sleep	slept	slept

Infinitive	Past Tense	Past Participle
slide	slid	slid
sling	slung	slung
smell	smelt, smelled	smelt, smelled
sow	sowed	sown, sowed
speak	spoke	spoken
speed	sped, speeded	sped, speeded
spell	spelt, spelled	spelt, spelled
spend	spent	spent
spill	spilt, spilled	spilt, spilled
spin	spun, span	spun
spit	spat	spat
split	split	split
spoil	spoilt, spoiled	spoilt, spoiled
spread	spread	spread
spring	sprang	sprung
stand	stood	stood
steal	stole	stolen
stick	stuck	stuck
sting	stung	stung
stride	strode	stridden, strid
strike	struck	struck (stricken)
swear	swore	sworn
sweep	swept	swept
swell	swelled	swollen, swelled
swim	swam	swum
swing	swung	swung
take	took	taken
teach	taught	taught
tear	tore	torn
tell	told	told
think	thought	thought
thrive	throve, thrived	thriven, thrived
throw	threw	thrown
thrust	thrust	thrust
tread	trod	trodden, trod
understand	understood	understood
undertake	undertook	undertaken
undo	undid	undone
upset	upset	upset
wake	woke, waked	woken, waked
wear	wore	worn
weave	wove	woven
wed	wedded, wed	wedded, wed
weep	wept	wept
win	won	won
wind	wound	wound
withdraw	withdrew	withdrawn
withhold	withheld	withheld
write	wrote	written

Appendix 6 Subject-Verb Concord

Note:	* Indicates that the sentence is incorrect.

1 The -s is often wrongly forgotten in the 3rd person singular of the present tense, i.e. *the stem + s*. E.g. *The student attend the language course and he study hard*. It should be *attends* and *studies*.

2 Frequently *has* and *have* are used wrongly, e.g. *The course have taught me a lot*. Here it should be *has*.

3 Mistakes are also made with *is* and *are*, and *was* and *were*, e.g. *Jose and Eduardo is from Mexico*; *Some students was late this morning*. It should be *are* and *were*.

4 Another common mistake is with *do* and *does*, especially in negative sentences, e.g. *He don't study Chemistry, he study Physics*. It should be *doesn't* (or *does not*) *study* and *studies*.

You must be careful to look at the subject of the verb, decide if it is singular or plural and then choose the appropriate verb form:
Stem + s, *has, is, was* or *does*, if singular (all end in -s).
stem, *have, are, were* or *do*, if plural.

Other points to note

5 Look at this sentence: *The number of students on the course is less than last year*.
Here the subject is *the number of students on the course* but the main word is *number*. Therefore the verb must be singular *is*.
Often a mistake is made by putting a plural verb (*are* in this case) because of the influence of a plural noun *students*.

6 Some nouns which are grammatically *singular* may be followed by a *plural* verb form. These are often called *collective nouns*. E.g. *The government have taken an important decision. The England football team were beaten by Italy. The class have a test on Friday*.

With collective nouns in their singular form it is usually possible to use either a singular verb or a plural verb. Therefore, *The government has taken . . . ; The England football team was beaten . . . ; The class has a test . . .* are equally correct.

7 Learn by heart these examples:

a *Almost always singular*
(i.e. verb in singular form): news, information, music, mathematics, phonetics, the United States, advice, evidence, accommodation, equipment.
e.g. The news *was* very good.

b *Usually singular*
aid, research.
e.g. His research *is* progressing very well.

   c *Always plural*

      (i.e. verb in plural form): people, police, cattle.

      e.g. The police *are* doing their best to control the traffic.

d *Singular and plural*

      (i.e. these words do *not* change; but the verb may be singular or plural according to the meaning): means, series, species, sheep, aircraft.

      e.g. The series of experiments that he conducted *was* very successful.

      Several species of butterfly *are* in danger of dying out.

Appendix 7   Comparisons

---

1 Formation

a The *regular comparative* and *superlative* of adjectives and adverbs is formed as follows:
  1 by adding the endings -*er* and -*est* to words with *one* syllable.
  2 by placing the words *more* and *most* in front of words with *three* or more syllables.

word length	adjective or adverb	comparative	superlative
one syllable	new soon	newer sooner	newest soonest
three syllables or more	easily convenient	more easily more convenient	most easily most convenient

1 words with *two syllables* may be like 1 or 2 above:
a Generally they will add the ending -*er* and -*est* if they end in:
    -*y* or -*ly* e.g. funny (funnier, funniest); friendly (friendlier, friendliest)
But Note: *adverbs* ending in -*ly* take *more* and *most*.
          e.g. quickly (more quickly, most quickly)
    -*ow*   e.g. narrow (narrower, narrowest)
    -*le*   e.g. able (abler, ablest)
    -*er*   e.g. clever (cleverer, cleverest)
b Most of the remaining words take *more* and *most*:
          e.g. careful (more careful, most careful)
c Some common two-syllable adjectives can have either type of comparison: common, handsome, polite, quiet.
          e.g. polite   politer   politest
                        more polite   most polite

b *Irregular comparison* is made by:
  1 a small group of very frequent adjectives:
      e.g. bad   worse   worst
            far   further/farther   furthest/farthest
            good   better   best
            many   more   most
  2 a small group of adverbs:
      e.g. badly   worse   worst
            far   further/farther   furthest/farthest
            little   less   least
            much   more   most
            well   better   best

2 Use in sentence constructions

There are a number of constructions using comparisons. Some of the commonest ones are shown below in sentences:

a Showing *equivalence* (i.e. the same)
1 Ann is *as* clever *as* Tom.
2 This book is *the same* price *as* that one.
3 There are *as many* students in this room *as* in the other one.
4 There is *as much* liquid in the first test-tube *as* in the second.

b Showing *non-equivalence* (i.e. not the same)
1 The medical library is *not as* / *so* } *big as* the science library.
2 John's essay was *longer than* Peter's.
3 However, Peter's essay was *more* carefully written *than* John's and contained *fewer* mistakes (*than* John's).
4 There were *not as many* students in the seminar *as* at the lecture.
5 The student did *not* do *as much* homework *as* his teacher had hoped.
6 This problem is *less* difficult *than* the previous one.

c Showing one item *compared* with a number (i.e. the superlative)
1 He scored *the highest* marks in the annual examination.
2 *The most convenient* time for him to see his tutor was in the early afternoon.
3 Some economists find that *the least* interesting part of their subject is statistics.

d Showing *parallel increase* (i.e. two comparatives)
The *bigger* the problem (was), the *more* interesting he found it.

Note: A common mistake is to confuse and mix some of the constructions, producing, for example, the *wrong* construction *more . . . as* which should be *more . . . than*.

117

Appendix 8   Connectives

The main connectives are grouped below according to the similarity of their meaning with the three basic connectives *and*, *or*, *but*. For information about their use in sentences, you should look in a good dictionary.

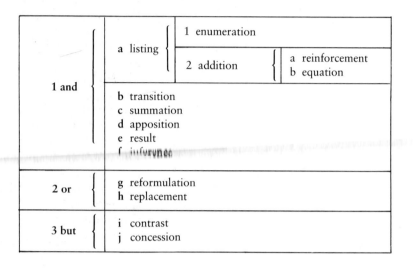

1 and	**a** listing	1 enumeration		
		2 addition	a reinforcement	
			b equation	
	b transition			
	c summation			
	d apposition			
	e result			
	f inference			
2 or	**g** reformulation			
	h replacement			
3 but	**i** contrast			
	j concession			

1 and

a **Listing:**
1 **Enumeration** indicates a *cataloguing* of what is being said. Most enumerations belong to clearly defined *sets*:

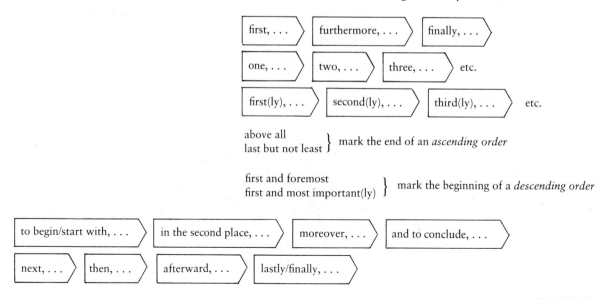

2 **Addition** to what has been previously indicated.
a *Reinforcement* (includes confirmation):

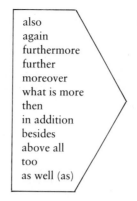

also
again
furthermore
further
moreover
what is more
then
in addition
besides
above all
too
as well (as)

b *Equation* (similarity with what has preceded):

equally
likewise
similarly
correspondingly
in the same way

Note:

a either
neither
nor
not only . . . (but) also . . .
neither . . . nor . . .
From the point of view of meaning these are often the
negative equivalents of *and*.
Neither leaves the series open for further additions, whereas *nor* concludes it.

b The truth of a previous assertion may be confirmed or
contradicted by:
indeed
actually
in (actual) fact
really
in reality

b **Transition** can lead to a new stage in the sequence of thought:

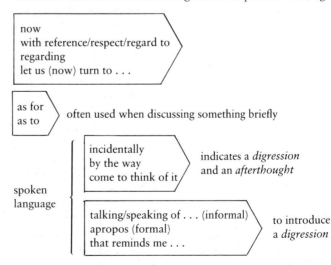

now
with reference/respect/regard to
regarding
let us (now) turn to . . .

as for
as to
often used when discussing something briefly

spoken
language

incidentally
by the way
come to think of it
indicates a *digression*
and an *afterthought*

talking/speaking of . . . (informal)
apropos (formal)
that reminds me . . .
to introduce
a *digression*

c **Summation** indicates a generalisation or summing-up of what has preceded:

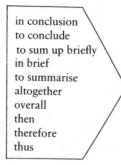

in conclusion
to conclude
to sum up briefly
in brief
to summarise
altogether
overall
then
therefore
thus

d **Apposition** used to refer back to previous sentences or to parallel or related references:

i.e., that is, that's to say
viz. namely
in other words
or, or rather, or better
and
as follows
e.g. for example, for instance, say, such as, including, included, especially, particularly, in particular, notably, chiefly, mainly, mostly (of)

Note: The relationships between sentences that are included are: *reformulation* (see **g** below), *exemplification* and *particularisation*

e **Result** expresses the consequence or result of what was said before:

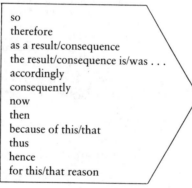

so
therefore
as a result/consequence
the result/consequence is/was . . .
accordingly
consequently
now
then
because of this/that
thus
hence
for this/that reason

f **Inference** indicates a deduction from what is implicit in the preceding sentence(s):

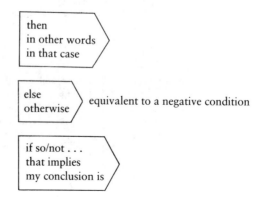

then
in other words
in that case

else
otherwise
equivalent to a negative condition

if so/not . . .
that implies
my conclusion is

2 or

g Reformulation to express in another way:

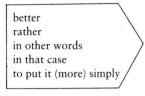

> better
> rather
> in other words
> in that case
> to put it (more) simply

h Replacement to express an alternative to what has preceded:

> again
> alternatively
> rather
> better/worse (still) . . .
> on the other hand
> the alternative is . . .
> another possibility would be

3 but

i Contrast with what has preceded:

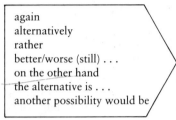

> instead
> conversely
> then
> on the contrary
> by (way of) contrast
> in comparison
> (on the one hand) . . . on the other hand . . .

j Concession indicates the unexpected, surprising nature of what is being said in view of what was said before:

besides	yet
(or) else	in any case
however	at any rate
nevertheless	for all that
nonetheless	in spite of/despite that
notwithstanding	after all
only	at the same time
still	on the other hand
while	all the same
(al)though	even if/though

Based upon Chapter 10: 'Sentence Connection', in A Grammar of Contemporary English *by Quirk, Greenbaum, Leech and Svartvik (Longman).*

Appendix 9 Referencing

1 Footnotes

A footnote is a note at the bottom (or foot) of a page in a book or journal: it is used to explain a word or other item, or to add some special information or a reference. Sometimes footnotes appear at the end of the essay or article, or even at the back of a book.

A small number is written above the word or item in the text. The explanation of the item is then given the same number. If there are two or more footnotes then they are numbered in sequence 1, 2, 3, etc. If they appear at the foot of each page, the numbering starts anew on each page. If they appear at the end of an essay, the numbering is continuous throughout the essay. There are several systems of giving footnotes but this is the simplest:

. . . has given rise to a school of thought called neo[1]-Marxism

---

[1] neo—a new or modern form or development of

2 Quotations

When referring to a book or article in an essay, the normal procedure is to give the author's surname, the year of publication in brackets, and the page numbers if possible. The full reference is then given at the end of the essay.

There are three basic ways of using quotations in an essay:

a quotation marks around the author's words which are then incorporated in the text: this is often used for short quotations:

. . . (Seers, 1979, pp. 27–28), a further dimension is added—"development now implies, inter alia, reducing cultural dependence on one or more of the great powers". Self reliance thus becomes . . .

b the quotation is indented (i.e. it starts further from the margin than the other lines—and it may be in a different type size or style; the quotation marks are usually omitted):

For Seers,
'Development' is inevitably a normative concept, almost a synonym for improvement. To pretend otherwise is just to hide one's value judgements.
(Seers, 1972, p. 22)

Posing the question . . .

c a paraphrase (i.e. rewriting the author's words):

Hicks and Streeten (1979, p. 568) identify and review four different approaches to the problem of measurement, namely: . . .

3 References and Bibliographies

References, at the end of an essay for example, are arranged in alphabetical order (a–z) of the author's surname or the name of the organisation. If more than one reference is given by the same author, then the earlier dated reference will appear first. If two or more references by the same author appear in the same year, they will be labelled in sequence with letters (a, b, c, etc.) after the year. References to one author are normally listed before those of joint authorship of the same author. E.g.

BIBLIOGRAPHY

Booth D. (1975) 'Andre Gunder Frank: an introduction and appreciation' in Oxaal I., Barnett T. and Booth D. (eds), *Beyond the Sociology of Development*, Routledge and Kegan Paul.

Cairncross A. and Puri M. (eds.) (1976), *Employment, Income Distribution and Development Strategy*, Macmillan.

Foxley A. (1976a), 'Redistribution of consumption: effects on production and employment' in Foxley (ed.) (1976b).

Foxley A. (ed.) (1976b), *Income Distribution in Latin America*, C.U.P.

Jolly R. (1976), 'Redistribution with growth' in Cairncross and Puri (eds.) (1976)

Murray T. (1973a), 'How helpful is the generalised system of preferences to developing countries?', *Economic Journal*, Vol. 83, No. 330

Murray T. (1973b), 'EEC enlargement and preferences for the developing countries', *Economic Journal*, Vol. 83, No. 331

Differences between references to books and journals

a Note the following sequence of information commonly used in references to *books*:

Author's surname, initials, (date—in brackets), *title* (underlined or in italics), place of publication, publisher. E.g.

Frank, A. C. (1967), *Capitalism and Underdevelopment in Latin America*, New York, Monthly Review Press.

b In references to articles in *journals* there are some differences in the information given:

Author's surname, initials, (date—in brackets), title of article, *name of journal* (underlined or in italics), volume number, issue number, sometimes season or month, sometimes page numbers. E.g.

Murray, R. Daniel and Smith, E. O. (1983). The role of dominance and intrafamilial bonding in the avoidance of close inbreeding. *Journal of Human Evolution*, 12, 5, 481–486.

Alphabetical order

It is important that references are arranged in strict alphabetical order. It is usually necessary to include the first names or initials of authors in addition to their surnames. Surnames beginning with *Mac* and *Mc* are placed together as *Mac*. E.g. *McKenzie* will come before *Madison*.

Test Yourself

The following 10 surnames (and initials) are those of authors of books. Arrange them correctly in strict alphabetical order from 1 to 10 in the spaces provided.

Dawson, E.	1	_____
Davidson, D.	2	_____
Davey, A. C.	3	_____
Davies, C. T.	4	_____
Day, D. A.	5	_____
Davey, A. M.	6	_____
Davis, A.	7	_____
Davidson, G. D.	8	_____
Davies, C. W.	9	_____
Davy, A.	10	_____

Now check your answers (page 144).

Appendix 10   Examination and Essay Questions: Glossary

Research has shown that, in general, there tend to be four main tasks that are required of students when they write essays in examinations. These are to show familiarity with:

1 a concept
2 the relations between/among concepts
3 a process
4 argumentation

There is considerable variation in the question types that are used. Remember that the question words may be qualified by words that follow, and thus the emphasis may be changed in the question. Also bear in mind that question words may have different meanings depending on the discipline in which they are used. Below are the most frequently used question types together with their possible meanings. It is possible to cross-reference some of the words for additional explanations e.g. *enumerate* has the meaning 'name and *list*'; *list* is then explained as 'put in sequence; catalogue; mention.'

question word	meaning
account for	give reasons for; explain
give an account of	describe
analyse	divide, describe, discuss, examine, explain
assess	decide the importance and give reasons
calculate	estimate; determine; weigh reasons carefully
characterise	describe
classify	arrange into groups
comment on	explain the importance of
compare	describe similarities
consider	think about carefully
contrast	describe differences
criticise	discuss and point out faults
deduce	conclude; infer
define	state precisely the meaning of; explain
demonstrate	show clearly by giving proof or evidence
describe	say what something is like
determine	find out something; calculate
differentiate between	show how something is different
discuss	consider something from different points of view, and then give your own opinion

question word	meaning
distinguish between	describe the difference between
elaborate	discuss in detail, with reasons and examples
elucidate	explain and make clear
enumerate	name and list, and explain
estimate	calculate; judge; predict
evaluate	assess and explain
examine	look at carefully; consider
explain	make clear; give reasons for
express	show, describe
identify	point out and describe
indicate	show, explain
infer	conclude something from facts or reasoning
illustrate	give examples that support your answer
justify	give good reasons for; explain satisfactorily
list	put in sequence; catalogue; mention
mention	describe briefly
name	identify
outline	give a short description of the main points
prove	show that something is true or certain; provide strong evidence (and examples) for

question word	meaning	question word	meaning
quantify	express or measure the amount or quantity of	state	express carefully, fully and clearly
relate	give an account of	summarise	give the main points of
show	indicate; give evidence of; make clear; demonstrate, illustrate	trace	outline and describe
speculate	form an opinion without having complete knowledge; suggest	verify	make sure that something is accurate or true; check
suggest	mention as a possibility; state as an idea for consideration; propose		

In addition, there are four other question words that are commonly used in conjunction with other words. These are: *how, what, which, why.*

e.g. 1 How far—to what extent
   2 What are the implications of—the suggested or long-term results of
     What is the significance of—the meaning and importance of
     What are the procedures—the method and order of doing something; the set of action necessary
   3 Which factors—what are the circumstances or conditions that bring about a result
   4 Why—for what reason; with what purpose

Look at some past examination papers for your subject. Draw up a list of the question types, noting in particular the ones that appear frequently. Using that as a basis, compile a glossary for your own subject area.

Key to Exercises and Notes

Answers are given where the choice is restricted.
Where the exercise is 'open' (several answers are possible),
teachers should check the answers carefully.

Unit 1   Key

Answers to the Exercises

Stage 2 (page 10)

Connectives
Exercise 1a
A choice of connectives from the list is possible, though
hence is less frequently used.
1 d   2 b   3 e

Exercise 1b
Many answers are possible. Suggested answers:
4   not many students were able to take notes.
5   it took him a long time to finish reading the English
text-book.

Exercise 2a
A choice of connectives from the list is possible, though *In
other words* is the most frequently used.
1 c   2 d   3 a

Exercise 2b
Many answers are possible. Suggested answers are:
4   she speaks English and French equally well.
5   if you have a sensitive 'ear' (or are sensitive to sound
changes) you will learn languages easily.

Exercise 3a
A choice of connectives from the list is possible, though
However is the most frequently used.
1 e   2 c   3 b

Exercise 3b
Many answers are possible. Suggested answers are:
4   to everyone's surprise, he passed it easily.
5   he insisted on continuing (with) it and completing it.

Unit 2   Key

Notes on the Exercises

Stage 1 (page 13)
1 and 3 'to' can have the meaning of 'in order to'
　　　　　e.g. . . . *to* whiten it
　　　　　　　. . . *to* flatten it
　　　　　　　. . . *to* soften it

Stage 2 (page 15)
1　　　The plural of *thesis* is *theses*
　　　　The University *of* X, or: X University
　　　　either: *of an* average *frequency of* X per term
　　　　　　or: *on* average X per term

In **1** the percentages total more than 100% because some students did more than one type of writing.

Phrases such as: 'the majority, just over half/50%, about one-third, less than a quarter', can be used or practised in relation to the table

Note: The description in this exercise is an *alternative* to using the table. For practice in using tables *and* language that comments on significant items within the tables, see *Unit 11: Interpretation of Data* (page 68).

Answers to the Exercises

Stage 1 (page 13)

1 a The following verbs should be underlined:
is stripped   are sawn   are conveyed   are placed   are cut   are mixed   are heated . . . crushed   is cleaned   is . . . bleached   is passed through   are produced   is removed   are pressed, dried . . . refined . . . is produced

2 c . . . are placed . . . are cut . . . which are mixed with . . . are heated and crushed . . . which is cleaned . . . is . . . bleached . . . is passed through . . . are produced . . . is removed . . . which are pressed, dried and refined . . . is produced.

3c The wheat is harvested from the field.
h The wheat grain is transported to the silos.
a It is stored in the silos.
f The grain is cooked to soften it.
e It is cut into thin strips.
b These are woven into biscuits.
d Each biscuit is baked until it is brown.
g It is packed ready to be eaten.

4d Glass *is made* from sand, limestone, and soda ash.
h <u>First</u>, these three minerals *are mixed* together in the right proportions.
b <u>Then</u>, sometimes broken glass *is added*.
g <u>Next</u>, this mixture *is heated* strongly in a furnace.
f <u>Then</u> glass *is produced*.
a <u>After this</u>, it *is shaped* into bottles in the mould.
c <u>Next</u>, the bottles are *reheated and cooled* to strengthen the glass.
e <u>Finally</u>, they are ready *to be used*.

Note: a choice of *sequence markers* is possible: see *Appendix 8: Connectives*, Section **1 a** (page 118).

1 sand   2 limestone   3 soda ash   4 broken glass   5 a furnace   6 the mould

Stage 2 (page 15)

1 A survey was conducted among *50* overseas postgraduate students at *Manchester University* (or: at *the* University *of* Manchester). The purpose of the survey was to discover the type, *frequency* and *length* of academic writing that was expected of the students by their supervisors or tutors. *34%* of the students *wrote* reports, of an *average frequency of* 2 per term, *of an* average length *of 4000 words*.

2a was carried out
b were distributed
c were requested
d were collected
e were analysed
f were published

Stage 3 (page 16)

2   The Stages of Writing an Essay

a Think	**j** Look	**r** Ask
b Understand	**k** Decide	**s** Revise
c Make	**l** Select	**t** Write
d Note	**m** Divide	**u** Make
e Add	**n** Write	**v** Remember
f Read	**o** Write	**w** Compile
g Write	**p** Avoid	**x** Ensure
h Keep	**q** Read	**y** Add
i Acknowledge		

3   Summary of the Stages of Writing an Essay
suggested answer (others may be possible):

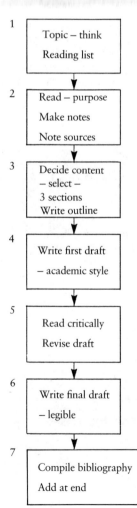

1   Topic – think
Reading list

2   Read – purpose
Make notes
Note sources

3   Decide content
– select –
3 sections
Write outline

4   Write first draft
– academic style

5   Read critically
Revise draft

6   Write final draft
– legible

7   Compile bibliography
Add at end

Unit 3   Key

Answers to the Exercises

Stage 1 (page 20)
1 1 The Atlantic Ocean   2 Scotland   3 Northern
Ireland   4 The Irish Republic (or: The Republic of
Ireland)   5 The North Sea   6 Wales   7 England
8 London   9 The English Channel   10 France

2 Alternatives are given in brackets:
(1) is surrounded by   (2) comprises (consists of; is
composed of)   (3) lies off   (4) consists of (is
composed of; comprises)   (5) is composed of
(consists of; comprises)   (6) is situated in (is located
in)   (7) was   (8) was (is)   (9) were (are)   (10) is . . .
spoken   (11) was spoken by   (12) spoke

Stage 2 (page 22)
1 Suggested answer (alternatives are possible):
Iceland is an island that lies close to the Arctic Circle. The
nearest country is Greenland which is 180 miles away and
from which Iceland is separated by the Denmark Strait.
The island is surrounded by the Atlantic Ocean, to the
south, and the Norwegian Sea, to the east. The capital city
is Reykjavik which is situated in south-west Iceland.

Iceland has a total area of 103,000 square kms. About
1% of the land area is cultivated (or: is devoted to
cultivation), about 25% is devoted to grassland and
vegetation, and 74% is glaciers, lava and wasteland. The
centre of Iceland (or: Inland Iceland) consists of mountains
and plateaus.

Iceland has a (generally) cool temperate and oceanic
climate. It has an annual rainfall of 80.5 cm.

In 1987 the (estimated) population of Iceland was
247,024. The density of population was (approximately)
2.5 people per square kilometre. In Iceland Icelandic is the
language which is spoken.

Unit 4   Key

Answers to the Excercises

Stage 1 (page 26)
2 Suggested notes:

E. C.

E.C. origins → May 9, 1950
↓
E.C.S.C. 1952
↓
Treaty of Rome (March 25, 1957)
↓
E.E.C.
(6 members: F, G, B, I, L, N)
↓
1973 + U.K., D, Rep of I.
+ 1980s = Gr., S, & P.

Stage 2 (page 27)

1 The United Nations
The *origins* of the U.N. can *be* traced back *to* the
League of Nations. This *was* an international *organisation*
which *was* created *by* the Treaty of Versailles *in* 1920 with
the purpose *of* achieving world peace. Before 1930, the
League, from its Geneva headquarters, *organised*
international conferences and did useful humanitarian
work. *However*, it failed *to* deal effectively *with*
international aggression *during* the 1930s. The League
was formally closed *in* 1946 and *was* superseded *by* the
United Nations.

The U.N was *founded* on 24th October, 1945, when
the U.N. Charter *was* ratified *by* the 51 founder member
countries. Almost *all* the countries of the *world* are now
members: 159 in all.

The U.N. was *established* to maintain international
peace, and to encourage international co-operation to
overcome economic, social, cultural and humanitarian
problems. Apart *from* the *principal* organs of the U.N.
(e.g. The General Assembly, The Security Council etc.),
most of the U.N.'s work is done *through* its specialised
bodies *and* agencies. *Some* of the best *known* are,
perhaps, the FAO, ILO, IMF, WHO, UNESCO and
UNICEF.

Stage 3 (page 29)

2	1	d	6	f
	2	j	7	a
	3	g	8	h
	4	i	9	e
	5	c	10	b

3 Suggested notes:

UNIVERSITIES IN ENGLAND

Oldest: Oxford 1185
↓ Cambridge 1209
London 1836
↓
c. 19th/20th — civic univs — industrial are
↓ (eg Manchester 1880, Birmingham
1940s/1950s — other civic univs
↓ (eg Nottingham 1948)
1960s largest expansion of univs —
parkland / green fields
(eg Kent, warwick 1965 —latest,
↓
1969 Open University

Unit 5   Key

Notes on the Exercises

1 When giving an extended definition of a subject it may be necessary to comment on some of the methods, processes, techniques, stages, steps, etc. involved, e.g.

> Moulding is one of the <u>methods</u> of *shaping* plastics.
> Polymerisation is the <u>process</u> *of turning* chemicals into plastics.

Notice that the form *of+verb+ing* is used here instead of the *wh*-word.

2 The biggest difficulty in writing a definition is to have a clear idea of the *concept* to be defined. This involves careful organisation of the necessary information. Finally, the language used to express the concept must be correctly selected.

3 In definitions it is often useful to give examples. This is the subject of Unit 6.

Answers to the Exercises

Stage 1 (page 33)

1a is an institution where
 b is a person who
 c is a metal which

2	1e	. . . a person who designs . . .
	2h	. . . an instrument which makes . . .
	3a	. . . a machine which produces . . .
	4g	. . . a person who studies . . .
	5j	. . . a geometric figure which has . . .
	6i	. . . a vegetable which is . . .
	7b	. . . a person who studies . . .
	8f	. . . a book which gives . . .

3a i 3   ii 1 (and perhaps 3)   iii 2
 b Various answers are possible. Suggestions:
 i   A lecturer is a person who teaches students in a college or university.
 ii   A dictionary is a book which explains the words of a language and is arranged in alphabetical order.
 iii A degree is an academic qualification which is given by a university to a student who has passed the appropriate examinations.

Stage 2 (page 35)

1 1 Plastics are substances which are moulded into shape when they are heated.

   2 A mineral is a structurally homogeneous solid of definite chemical composition which is formed by the inorganic process of nature.

   3 Rayons are man-made fibres produced from wood.

   4 A fossil is an organic trace buried by natural processes and subsequently permanently preserved.

2a 1 Demography is the study of population growth and its structure.

   2 Zoology is the science of the structure, forms and distribution of animals.

   3 Biology is the science of the physical life of animals and plants.

b 1 Sociology may be defined as the science which studies the nature and growth of society and social behaviour.

   2 Theology may be defined as the study of religious beliefs and theories.

   3 Astronomy may be defined as the science of the sun, moon, stars and planets.

Stage 3 (page 36)

1 1 Criminal psychology may be defined as the branch of psychology which investigates the psychology of crime and of the criminal.

   2 Chemistry may be defined as the branch of science which deals with the composition and behaviour of substances.

   3 Social economics may be defined as the branch of economics which is concerned with the measurement, causes and consequences of social problems.

Unit 6 Key

Notes on the Exercises

1 There are several ways of referring to *examples*, not just the expression 'for example' or 'e.g.' (although these are the most common).

   It is safer not to use *as* or *like* as they can easily be used wrongly.

2 When using *such as* (or the alternative forms) be careful to give only examples and *not* the complete set, group or list. For example, if we agree that there are 4 language skills (listening, speaking, reading, writing) then the following sentence would be *wrong*:

   The language skills, for example listening, speaking, reading and writing, need to be practised. (wrong)

However, it would be correct to put:

   The language skills, for example speaking and writing, need to be practised.

3 Note the difference between the following abbreviations (which are sometimes confused):

   e.g. = for example (some examples from a list are given)

   i.e. = that is (to say); in other words.
           e.g. *males, i.e. men and boys* . . .

   viz. = namely; it is/they are.
           e.g. *There are 4 language skills, viz. listening, speaking, reading and writing.*

4 Notice the use of the *colon* (:) and the *comma* (,) in listing examples in **Stage 1, 1** *What is language?*

5 Be careful in **Stage 3, 1** *Writing Systems* not to use 'for example' or 'such as' wrongly. It would be *wrong* to say: 'There are three main writing systems, *for example*, word syllabic, syllabic and alphabetic . . .' (because the *total* number is three and here 'for example' lists *all* of them instead of only some).

6 Description, definition and exemplification are closely linked. So also is classification: this is in Unit 7.

Answers to the Exercises

Stage 1 (page 38)

1 a and **b**

What is language?

A language is a signalling system which operates with symbolic vocal sounds, and which is used by a group of people for the purposes of communication.

Let us look at this definition in more detail because it is language, more than anything else, that distinguishes man from the rest of the animal world.

Other animals, it is true, communicate with one another by means of cries: for example, many birds utter warning calls at the approach of danger; apes utter different cries, such as expressions of anger, fear and pleasure. But these various means of communication differ in important ways from human language. For instance, animals' cries are not articulate. This means, basically, that they lack structure. They lack, for example, the kind of structure given by the contrast between vowels and consonants. They also lack the kind of structure that enables us to divide a human utterance into words.

We can change an utterance by replacing one word in it by another: a good illustration of this is a soldier who can say, e.g. "tanks approaching from the north", or he can change one word and say "aircraft approaching from the north" or "tanks approaching from the west"; but a bird has a single alarm cry, which means "danger!"

This is why the number of signals that an animal can make is very limited: the great tit is a case in point; it has about twenty different calls, whereas in human language the number of possible utterances is infinite. It also explains why animal cries are very general in meaning.

2 1 an example   2 such as   3 for instance (*or* for example)   4 for example (or: for instance)   5 illustration   6 a case in point.

Stage 2 (page 39)

(In these exercises different choices of languages are possible.)

1a 1 There are a number of languages which are descended from Latin: for example, Provençal and Catalan.

2 There are a number of languages, such as Provençal and Catalan, which are descended from Latin.

b 1 There are a number of languages which are descended from Sanskrit: for example, Bengali and Hindi.

2 There are a number of languages, such as Bengali and Hindi, which are descended from Sanskrit.

2a An example of such a family is the Germanic group of languages. Examples of members of the family are English and German.

b An example of such a family is the Sino-Tibetan group of languages. Examples of members of the family are Thai and Chinese.

Stage 3 (page 40)

1 The following is a suggestion: some variations are possible.

Writing Systems

Writing may be defined as a (the) method of human intercommunication by means of conventional visible marks. There are three main writing systems: firstly, word-syllabic, in which one sign represents one word, for example, Chinese. Secondly, syllabic, in which one sign represents one syllable; examples are Amharic and Japanese. Finally, alphabetic, in which one sign represents one sound; Greek, Latin and Arabic are examples of this system.

Unit 7   Key

Notes on the Exercises

Stage 1 (page 42)

Note: a It is 'divided *into*' (*not* divided to)
 b The spelling is '*divided*' and 'gramma*r*'
 c Remember: *criterion* = singular, *criteria* = plural

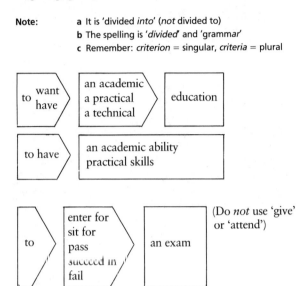

(Do *not* use 'give' or 'attend')

Stage 2 (page 44)

Note: a *genus* = singular, *genera* = plural.
 b *Species* is the same form for singular or plural. In the singular it can be used thus: '*A species is* . . .'
 c It is not necessary to fully understand the technical vocabulary for describing birds: it is more important to be able to use the general language of classification.

Stage 3 (page 45)

1 It is important to remember that in order to classify there must be clearly recognisable *criteria* (e.g. age, size, number of employees).

2 The criteria being used in the classification may be stated at the very beginning, as the choice of criteria determines which items are placed in which group, class, etc. This may be done in a simple way, e.g.
 'X may be classified according to Y' (Y = the criterion)
or in a more complex way. E.g:
 'In classifying industrial enterprises by size, various criteria may be used. One is the amount of fixed assets, another the value of annual production and a third the number of employees. Each of these criteria of classification has some advantages and some drawbacks . . .'
(Then a discussion with examples follows.)

(From "Small Industry in the Underdeveloped Countries" by B. F. Hoselitz, in *Economic Policy for Development*, edited by I. Livingstone, Penguin 1971).

Note: If more practice is needed in classifying items, or if a discussion is required, or a group working together with a teacher writing on the blackboard, the following subjects might be used: animals, trees, transport, vehicles, energy, heat, newspapers, sports or games.

Answers to the Exercises

Stage 1 (page 42)

1a . . . can/may be classified according to . . .
 b . . . two types of . . .
 c . . . can/may be sub-divided . . .
 d . . . may be grouped according to . . .
 e . . . an examination (at 11 years).

2 1 e   2 b   3 g   4 a   5 f   6 d   7 c

3a *Diagram 1: State Schools in England and Wales*

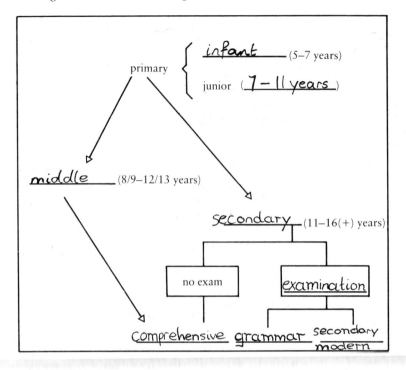

b Suggested brief description:

There are two types of school: primary and secondary. Primary schools can be sub-divided, according to age, into infant schools and junior schools. Infant schools cater for children aged 5–7 and junior schools for children aged 7–11.

Secondary schools are for children 11–16+ years and may be grouped according to whether or not an exam is taken at the age of 11. If there is no exam children proceed to a comprehensive school. If there is an exam children proceed to a grammar school or a secondary modern school, depending on their results in the exam.

Stage 2 (page 45)

2 *Diagram 2: The Classification of Birds*

Classification divisions or categories	Example of classification of *Golden Eagle* for each division	Number of the divisions
ORDER	FALCON-LIKE	27
FAMILY	FALCON	215
GENUS	EAGLE	–
SPECIES	GOLDEN EAGLE	8514

3a A bird is a creature (or animal) which has two wings, feathers, two legs, a toothless bill, warm blood, and can lay eggs. (It is usually able to fly.)

b A species is an interbreeding group of birds which do not normally mate with other such groups.

c 1 If the feet are designed so that they can grip a perch.

 2 If they are song-birds.

d Sparrows and crows.

e 1 *families*: external characteristics such as the shape of the beak and feet, and the colour pattern of the feathers.

 2 *orders*: features such as the structure of the skull, the arrangement of the muscles in the legs, and the condition of the young at the time of hatching.

4 There are 27 main orders of birds, for example, falcon-like birds. Each order may be divided into families, such as falcons, and each family may be sub-divided into genera: eagles are an example. Finally, each genus may be further sub-divided into a number of species, e.g. golden eagle.

Stage 3 (page 45)

1a Whether or not the drinks are alcoholic.

 Whether or not the drinks are hot or cold.

 Whether or not the drinks are aerated.

b Suggested answer:

Drinks may be classified into two main groups: alcoholic and non-alcoholic.

Alcoholic drinks may be divided into spirits, wine, and beer. Non-alcoholic drinks may be divided into hot and cold drinks. Examples of hot drinks are tea, coffee, and cocoa. Cold drinks may be grouped according to whether or not they are aerated. Lemonade, tonic water, soda water and Coca-Cola are examples of aerated drinks. Non-aerated drinks may be (sub-) divided into squashes, fruit juice, and others.

Unit 8 Key

Notes on the Exercises

Stage 1 (page 49)

1a in *Table 2* the months, in order, are:

Janury, February, March, April, May, June, July, August, September, October, November, December.

 b A common error in using comparative forms is to confuse some of the items, e.g. *more . . . than* is sometimes confused with *as much as* and the *wrong* form 'more . . . as' is produced.

 c Care should also be taken not to confuse other items, e.g.

more people
a lot more people } do *not* write 'a lot *of* more people'
a lot of people

Stage 2 (page 50)

2a The letter might start:

Thank you for your letter (of date) in which you ask for some information about English dictionaries.

 b The recommendation might take these forms:

I recommend you to buy X . . .
In my opinion Y is the book to buy . . .
If I were you I would buy Z . . .
I would advise you to buy X . . .

 c The letter might conclude:

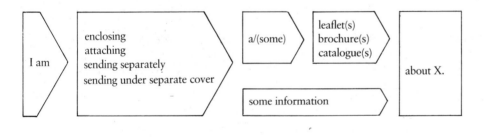

and to a friend it might end:

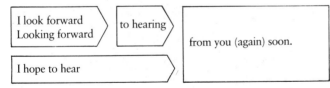

Stage 3 (page 53)

Generally, this stage provides some practice in using connectives, especially when contrasting items.

It is important that unrelated items should *not* be contrasted, e. g. do *not* compare temperature and religion.

Answers to the Exercises

Stage 1 (page 49)

1. 1 Longer than
   2 not so/nearly as . . . as
   3 the longest
   4 shorter than/not so long as
   5 the longest
   6 colder . . . than
   7 warmer/hotter/wetter . . . than
   8 more . . . than
   9 most . . . the wettest
   10 not so/nearly as . . . as
   11 the driest/the coldest
   12 the same as/as low as
   13 as . . . as
   14 less than
   15 hottest/wettest . . . the wettest/the hottest

Stage 2 (page 50)

1 **Note:** Other answers would be possible for some of these sentences if the instruction had not said 'use each word only once'.

a more . . . than
b greater . . . than
c as many . . . as
d most
e The same . . . as

f least
g Not so many . . . as
h as much . . . as
i More . . . than
j biggest

2 Various replies are possible but they will probably include reference to: more/fewer items, bigger/smaller, higher/lower price, more expensive (dearer), cheaper, more economical, better value.

Unit 9 Key

Notes on the Exercises

It is not possible here to practise all the combinations of connectives and constructions: there are a large number for all the cause-effect relationships. However, the *Structure and Vocabulary Aid* (page 60) illustrates some of the main constructions.

It may be useful to remember that the following questions relate to cause-effect relations:

What caused X?
What was the effect of X?
Why did X happen?

In **Stage 2, 2** and **3** notice the difference in use between e.g. cross*ing* and cross*ed*.

Answers to the Exercises

Stage 1 (page 56)

1. 1 d   4 f
   2 i   5 h
   3 g   6 c

2 A variety of connectives are possible. Check carefully with the *Structure and Vocabulary Aid* (page 60) to see if particular connectives etc. fit into the particular patterns shown here. Suggested answers:

a Because he worked hard he passed his examination.

b Prolonged illness is often caused by delayed treatment.

c The strike was caused by bad labour relations.

d The laboratory specimens were killed as a result of the fluctuation in temperature.

e That bottle must be handled very carefully as there is acid in it.

Stage 2 (page 58)

1 *Table 1: Climate*

Cause	Connective or Marker	Effect
rising temperatures	have been causing	2 the snowline to retreat on mountains all over the world. e.g. In Peru it has risen as much as 2,700 feet in 60 years.
—	As a result of this	3 vegetation has also been changing. e.g. In Canada, the agricultural cropline has shifted 50 to 100 miles northward.
—	has also been affected	4 The distribution of wildlife e.g. many European animals moving northwards into Scandinavia.
the melting of glaciers	(largely) due to	5 The sea has been rising at a rapidly increasing rate, e.g. in the last 18 years it has risen by about 6 inches

2 A variety of answers are possible. The most likely ones are listed below.

(1) caused/resulted in/led to (2) because/as/since (3) because of/as a result of/due to/on account of/owing to/through (4) consequently,/Therefore,/As a result/Because of this/etc./ (5) caused/resulted in/led to (6) cause of/reason for

Unit 10   Key

Notes on the Exercises

1 The different columns in the Scale of Qualification in the *Structure and Vocabulary Aid* (page 66) need to be looked at and carefully compared.

It would be useful to look again at the *Structure and Vocabulary Aid* to Unit 8, (Qualification of Comparison, page 54)

2 Reference is made in Stage 2 to *predictive statements* or *predictions*. Such generalised comments are based upon past experience and information. You can see, therefore, that there may be a close link between the past and the future (this will be important for verb tenses).

Answers to the Exercises

Stage 1 (page 63)

b

Quantity	Frequency	Probability
all minority majority a little most a number	usually seldom generally	possible undoubtedly likely will not definitely

Stage 2 (page 63)

1a Some flexibility is possible with the answers but there should be a *range* of *quantity* qualifications used, e.g. most, the majority of, many, (a) few.

b A *range* of *probability* qualifications will need to be used, e.g. probable, likely, possible, unlikely. Each one may be further qualified if necessary by adding 'very' in front of it.

2 Some variation is possible with the quantity qualifications but the answers should be similar to these:

A *minority of* students were *rarely* able to obtain their course books from libraries.
The majority of . . . sometimes . . .
A *number of . . .   often . . .*
A *few . . .   always . . .*

Stage 3 (page 64)

1 The following words should be underlined. They are given here in the order in which they appear in the text.

may	can be	seem
possible	perhaps	can be
can be	may	necessarily
may	tend to	possible
may be	may	suggest
often	often	It appears
suggests	most frequently	can be
may		do not seem

Unit 11   Key

Notes on the Exercises

This unit is useful for practising different expressions associated with visual information, viz. histogram, chart, graph, table.

Stage 1 (page 68)

1 The plural of *axis* is *axes*

2 It is *wrong* to write 'from *the* Chart 1': it should be either: 'from Chart 1' or 'from the chart'.

3 The organisation of information is important. Normally there is a progression from *big* to *small* (or vice-versa), or a *big/small contrast*. Sequencing markers or connectives may be used (i.e. first, next, then, followed by, finally).

4 In *Chart 1* the approximate percentages are:

Note: In 1986 only 7% of secondary school age pupils went to independent/private/fee-paying schools

Pupils in state secondary schools in England and Wales (%)

type of school \ year	1966	1971	1975	1980	1986
Technical (and other)	10	7	2	1	–
Grammar	25	20	8	4	3
Modern	55	38	20	7	4
Comprehensive	10	35	70	87	92

Stage 2 (page 69)

1a Useful introductory phrases:
   During the period 1874–1987. . . .
   From 1874 to 1987. . . .
   Since 1874. . . .
   For over a hundred years, from 1874 to 1987. . . .

Note: 'to solemnise' = to perform a religious ceremony

b Approximate calculations:
Church of England/Wales
1874 = 750 } *a fall of 405*
1987 = 345 } (per 1,000)

civil ceremonies
1874 = 100 } *an increase of 378*
1987 = 478 } (per 1,000)

Total marriages:
1874 = 850
1987 = 823

2a In this exercise verbs will either be in the future tense or will involve a qualification of probability.

It is, perhaps, necessary to comment that we assume that the trends shown in the graph will continue in a similar way. There is, however, a complication. The general trend is for weddings by civil ceremony to increase and for Church of England/Wales marriages to decline. Nevertheless, during the 1980s, there has been a slight reversal of this trend.

b On the basis of the figures calculated in **1** above we can say that for civil ceremonies there is an increase of 33 every 10 years, and for Church of England/Wales marriages there is a decline of 36 every 10 years. It is just over 30 years from 1987 to 2020 so we could calculate the trend according to these figures. But – these figures are based on an analysis of the *whole* period (from 1874 to 1987). It might be more realistic to base the future trend on data from the 1960s, 1970s and 1980s. The basis of any calculations used in predicting a trend should be indicated in the answer.

Stage 3 (page 70)
Different visual information is provided in order to give further practice. Only the most significant/interesting items should be commented on.

For an *additional exercise* in trends, the Stage 1 chart of pupils in secondary schools could be described, showing the trends of the different types of school over the 20-year period.

Answers to the Exercises

Stage 1 (page 69)

3 As can be seen from the chart, a larger percentage of secondary school pupils were at secondary modern schools than at any other kind of school in 1966. In fact, secondary modern schools accounted for as much as 55% of the pupils. On the other hand, technical (and other) schools accounted for only 10%. Comprehensive schools, also, accounted for only 10%.

4 There are various ways in which this may be answered. Mention should be made of the reversal in positions of comprehensive schools in 1986 compared with grammar schools, compared with both their positions in 1966. Two-and-a-half times as many pupils went to grammar schools in 1966 as went to comprehensive schools. By 1986 more than thirty times as many went to comprehensive schools as went to grammar schools.

Stage 2 (page 70)

2 A number of answers are possible. The suggestion below is for guidance. As can be seen from the graph, during the period 1874–1987, there was a marked decline in the proportion of marriages which were solemnised (or conducted) by the Church of England/Wales. They fell from 750 per 1,000 marriages in 1874 to 345 in 1987. Thus, there was a fall of 405 during the period.

On the other hand, there was a gradual increase in the proportion of marriages which were solemnised by a civil ceremony. These marriages accounted for only 100 per 1,000 in 1874 but rose to 478 in 1987. Thus, there was an increase of 378 during the period.

Note: Comment can also be made on the differences in the slopes of the two curves over different periods in the 113 years, particularly during the 1980s.

Unit 12   Key

Notes on the Exercises

Stage 1 (page 73)
All four paragraphs are possible introductions. Personal preference will play some part in the choice.

a The first paragraph is very short and, perhaps, does not tell us much. It is not good style to put 'of course' in the first sentence.

b The second paragraph certainly lists the problems. It is interesting to read but for academic writing, perhaps, a little too dramatic – almost like journalese. Some would say that it is too repetitive – three instances of 'it faces problems' – though others would say this is deliberate and adds emphasis to the point.

c The third paragraph gives more information but, for an introduction, perhaps, includes too much background on historical information before saying what the essay will include.

d The fourth paragraph will be considered by some to be the best as it sets out precisely, and in sequence, what the essay will include (with linking words – 'starting with . . . then . . . after this . . . finally . . .').

Unit 13   Key

Notes on the Exercises

The exercises in this unit can be used for revising some of the language functions practised in earlier units, e.g. definitions (what is *infant mortality?*), exemplification, comparison and contrast.

Stage 1 (page 78)

1 In order to be able to draw realistic conclusions, we normally need to have information about causes, reasons, etc. For example, Chart 1: *Unit 11 Stage 1, Pupils in state secondary schools in England and Wales* (page 68) we cannot, just from the chart, draw any conclusion about the large expansion in the number of pupils in comprehensive schools. We would need to know that it was British government educational policy at the time to promote the growth of comprehensive schools.

2 It may be of interest to see how the writer concluded the passage *Advantages and Disadvantages of the Lecturing Method* in *Unit 12 Stage 1* (page 75). The survey was concluded thus:

'An aspect of lecturing rarely, if ever, mentioned by its critics is its efficiency. With the aid of microphones and closed-circuit television it is possible to reach large audiences within one building; and, as we know from national television, lectures of great interest, employing expensive visual aids and a high standard of preparation, can be made available to millions. Moreover, video-tapes may enable other audiences to see and discuss the same programmes subsequently at times convenient in their own courses. Had there been little else to say in their favour, these advantages of economy and availability would certainly ensure their continuation, but even without the aid of television, lecturing is still an economical method.'

Notice the use of *inversion* at the beginning of the final sentence ('Had . . .') in order to achieve greater emphasis.

Note: *calorie* = a measure used when stating the amount of heat or energy that food will produce.
protein = a substance that helps to build up the body and keep it healthy.
kg. = kilogram   *lb.* = pound (weight)   *oz.* = ounces.

Stage 2 (page 79)
1 *infant mortality rate* = deaths of infants under one year old are expressed as a proportion (per thousand) of all live births in a given year.

(Note the spelling of *mortality*: do not confuse it with *morality*.)

population per hospital bed = the number of people in a country for every hospital bed, i.e. a ratio.

physician = doctor/surgeon
The concept of a *correlation* can be utilised here. A correlation is a shared relationship or causal connection between items, e.g. There is a *high correlation* between unemployment and crime.

2 The *cause* of the accidents is not given.

Answers to the Exercises

Stage 1 (page 79)
2b There is some flexibility in the answers. However, they should be similar to the following.
 . . . people in the U.S.A. have a (more than) sufficient daily intake of calories and protein.
 . . . those in India have a (barely) sufficient daily intake of protein but an insufficient (or inadequate) daily intake of calories.

Stage 2 (page 80)
1b Some possible conclusions, or types of conclusion, are as follows:

It can be concluded that there is a high correlation between protein intake and life expectancy.

It can be concluded that there is a close link between low intake of calories and protein and life expectancy; also, between poor medical facilities and infant mortality and life expectancy.

It can also be concluded that there seems to be a high correlation between medical facilities on the one hand, and infant mortality and life expectancy on the other.

Unit 14   Key

Answers to the Exercises

Stage 1 (page 82)
2 Several alternatives are possible. The main ones are given below.

(1) studying	(12) following/understanding
(2) (any subject)	(13) lecturers
(3) (any department)	(14) very
(4) consists	(15) to finish/in finishing
(5) dissertation	(16) much
(6) started	(17) slowly
(7) beginning	(18) forward
(8) submitted	(19) learning/remembering
(9) have learned	(20) However
(10) had	(21) as/because
(11) first	(22) thought of/decided on/chosen

Stage 2 (page 83)
1 A number of alternatives are possible.

(1) at
(2) start/begin/pursue/continue
(3) studying/preparing
(4) between
(5) supervisor/tutor/professor
(6) advised/asked/recommended/wanted (told)
(7) chosen/selected
(8) discussion(s)/meetings/consultation
(9) step/task/aim
(10) for
(11) advice/suggestion/recommendation
(12) item/topic/text/publication/reference
(13) bibliography/file/collection
(14) save
(15) end
(16) continued/spent/been
(17) research/thesis
(18) specifically/literature/further
(19) found/discovered/realised
(20) relevant/related/helpful
(21) progress
(22) anticipated/expected/predicted/planned/assumed
(23) group/meeting/number/team
(24) satisfied/pleased/happy/impressed
(25) provoked/stimulated/raised/encouraged

Stage 3 (page 84)
2 1 m   2 h   3 c   4 l   5 g   6 n   7 d   8 k   9 i
 10 a   11 e   12 j   13 f   14 b

Appendix 1 Key

Spelling Key (page 95)

1 C	6 B	11 C	16 C	21 B	26 B	31 B	36 A
2 B	7 C	12 A	17 A	22 C	27 D	32 B	37 B
3 C	8 D	13 D	18 C	23 D	28 A	33 D	38 D
4 B	9 D	14 B	19 D	24 D	29 C	34 C	39 D
5 D	10 A	15 B	20 D	25 A	30 A	35 B	40 C

If you get more than 3 answers wrong in Exercise 1, do the following exercise

Exercise 1a Do this additional spelling exercise in the same way as Exercise 1.

	A	B	C	D
1 AGENCIES	agences	agencies	agancies	agiences
2 ARGUES	argus	arguse	aruges	argues
3 BOUGHT	bougth	bough	bought	bougt
4 DIFFICULTIES	difficultes	difculties	difficulties	diffculties
5 FRIENDS	freinds	frends	friens	friends
6 HUNDRED	hunderd	hundred	handred	hundered
7 IMPORTANCE	importence	important	importance	importanse
8 QUESTIONNAIRE	questionnaire	questionnare	questionair	qestionnaire
9 RECIPIENT	recipent	recepient	recipeint	recipient
10 USEFULNESS	usefulnes	usefullness	usefulness	usfulness

Now check your answers carefully below. Then continue with Exercise 2.

Exercise 1a

10 C	6 B	3 C
9 D	5 D	2 D
8 A	4 C	1 B
7 C		

Exercise 2

1 achieve	4 insufficient	7 medicine
2 frequently	5 interviewed	8 research
3 increasingly	6 maintaining	9 referring
		10 successful

Exercise 3

1 separately	4 recommendation	7 embarrassed
2 preferred	5 environment	8 precede (or: proceed)
3 receive	6 consciousness	9 discussion
		10 characteristics

Punctuation Key (page 97)

Exercise 1

The first of the great civic universities established in England, Manchester is, today, the largest unitary university in the United Kingdom and an internationally famous centre of learning and research. It is well-endowed with resources and facilities. (or): The University Library, for instance, is one of the four big academic libraries in the country, and the University has its own modern theatre, television studios, art gallery, museum, shopping centre and, of course, extensive sports facilities.

Note: Do not look at the following until you have completed Exercise 2.

Exercise 2

Alternative punctuation is given in brackets.

Mr(.) Brown had been teaching English abroad for a number of years. He had forgotten how cold it could be in England in the winter.(:) It was often dull and grey in November(.) but it could be really cold in December, January(,) and February.(;) Even in the spring it could snow.(!) Mr(.) Brown looked out of the window(.) as the train crossed the River Avon.(,) He remembered the weather forecast that he had heard on the B(.)B(.)C(.) at 9 o'clock that Tuesday morning:(.) it had said that it would be wet and windy in the north-west. Manchester, where he was now travelling to, was, unfortunately, in the north-west(!)

For guidance on punctuation and the use of capital letters turn to *Appendix 3: Punctuation and Capital Letters* (page 107).

Grammar Key (page 98)

1a Table 3 <u>shows</u> that most of <u>these</u> accidents <u>occur</u> to young children.

Note: 1 The present continuous tense (*is showing*) is often wrongly used for the present simple tense (*shows*)

2 *This* is singular and should only be used with singular nouns. *These* is the plural form and should be used with nouns in the plural form.

3 The subject of the verb is *most . . . accidents* – it is plural and therefore needs the third person plural form of the present simple tense (*occur*).

b Each worker <u>pays</u> a small <u>amount of money</u> which is taken from <u>his</u> salary.

Note: 1 The final 's' is very often forgotten in the third person singular of the present simple tense.

2 *Money* is an uncountable noun (the indefinite article *a* cannot be used alone with it). We can either write *a small amount of money* or *some money* (or *a little money*).

3 *Salary* relates to *worker* which is singular; therefore, the possessive adjective must be used in the singular (*his*).

c Specialist doctors in hospitals <u>can be divided</u> into surgeons <u>who</u> operate <u>on</u> the body and (<u>other</u>) specialists <u>who</u> act as consultants.

Note: 1 The intransitive verb should be used in a passive tense here: notice the ending with *-ed*.

2 *Surgeons* and *specialists* are people, therefore the relative pronoun *who* must be used (*which* is used for inanimate objects and animals, not people).

3 The verb *operate* is followed by the preposition *on* when it has the meaning of 'perform a surgical operation' (on somebody).

4 *Another* is singular and normally has the meaning of 'one other'. It cannot be used immediately next to a plural noun. *Other* may be used before singular and plural countable nouns and before uncountable nouns.

d The number of schools <u>grew</u> gradually till 1965 and then the number <u>rose</u> suddenly.

Note: 1 The verb 'to grow' has irregular past tense and past participle forms: *grew, grown*.

2 The definite article *the* must be inserted: it refers back to *schools* at the beginning of the sentence.

3 The verb 'to rise' has irregular past tense and past participle forms: *rose, risen*.

e When a country <u>applies</u> for foreign <u>aid</u>, it is because it has <u>not</u> enough resources of its own.

Note: 1 The final 's' is needed for this third person singular, present simple tense. When the verb ends in the letter 'y' and the letter immediately in front of it is a consonant letter, the 'y' is changed to 'i' and 'es' is then added.

2 *Aid* meaning 'help' is an uncountable noun and must therefore be used in the singular form (even though it may have a plural *meaning*). Some other similar uncountable nouns are: *information, advice, research, evidence*.

3 A subject pronoun is needed: it is sometimes called impersonal *it*. Similarly the impersonal *there* is often wrongly omitted.

4 The usual negative form with the verb is *not. No* can often be used if the negative idea is closely linked with a noun. Here it is linked with *enough*. (*It has no resources of its own* would be possible. In this sentence *no* has the meaning of *not any*.)

2a If somebody <u>becomes</u> ill, then <u>he</u> can go to <u>a/the</u> local doctor.

Note: 1 The final 's' is needed for third person singular, present simple tense.

2 A subject pronoun is needed.

3 An article is needed: *the* is used if one particular local doctor is thought of or if only one exists.

b <u>In</u> my opinion, there <u>are</u> many <u>parents who</u> did not take care <u>of</u> their children.

Note: 1 The preposition *in* must be used in this set phrase.

2 The subject *parents* should clearly be plural.

3 The verb (*are*) should also be plural in order to agree.

4 The relative pronoun *who* is needed for people.

5 The verb is 'to take care *of*', meaning 'to be responsible for'.

c On the other hand, if we look at the table of accidents, we will see these facts.

Note: 1 *On* must be used in this set phrase. It is used to indicate contrasted points of view, arguments etc. (*on the one hand*, . . . *on the other hand*).
2 *At* is commonly used with the verb 'look'; here it has the meaning of 'examine'.
3 The plural form *these* is needed to 'agree' with *facts*. Or we can change it to the singular: *this fact*.

d In my country we have another kind of system; it is bigger and better.

Note: 1 *Other* would only be possible here if we put *the* in front of it; this would then suggest that there were two alternative systems. (In the plural this would become: . . . *other kinds* of systems; they are bigger and better.)

2 *Better* is already the comparative form of 'good' (the superlative is 'best'). *More* is only used to form the comparative of adjectives or adverbs with two or more syllables e.g. more logical, more comfortable; more quickly. (We could say *much* better.)

e The problem was solved by the introduction of machinery (or machines).

Note: 1 The past simple passive tense is being used: thus the ending *-ed* is necessary.
2 *Machinery* is uncountable. Alternatively the plural word *machines* may be used.

General Note: If you had any difficulty, turn to the Appendices at the end of this book (page 93). They may help you.

Vocabulary Key (page 99)

3 Exercise
a made (*or* makes. Other tenses of *make* are possible)
b done
c told (other tenses of *tell* are possible)
d borrow
e raised
f rose (possibly, though unusually, *was raised*)
g advice; choose
h mathematics; politics; logical; latter

Style and Appropriateness Key (page 101)

3 Exercise

a Formal	d Formal	g Informal
b Informal	e Formal	h Formal (Informal)
c Informal	f Formal	i Formal
		j Informal

5 Exercise
a It will also appear in the development of institutions . . .
b The ideal of economic development is associated with different policy goals . . .
c Greater clarity can be brought to the meaning of economic development . . .

Appendix 9   Key

Alphabetical Order Key (page 124)

3 1 Davey, A.C.
   2 Davey, A.M.
   3 Davidson, D.
   4 Davidson, G.D.
   5 Davies, C.T.
   6 Davies, C.W.
   7 Davis, A.
   8 Davy, A.
   9 Dawson, E.
   10 Day, D.A.